Sustainability in High-Excellence Italian Food and Wine

This book presents contemporary case studies on selected Italian food and wine products to explore how traditional production and consumption models address and adapt to the sustainability challenges in the Italian high-excellence agri-food sector.

Sustainability in High-Excellence Italian Food and Wine adopts a transaction cost economics approach, which is applied to five case-study chapters, each focusing on a key Italian agri-food product: Parmigiano Reggiano, Mozzarella di Bufala Campana, Amarone wine, Prosecco wine, and Prosciutto di San Daniele. The production and organization of these products face many challenges as they seek to balance competing priorities around economic viability, maintenance of high-quality standards and environmental and social impacts. The book argues that the development of sustainable and quality models requires changes to the structure and organization of the supply chain while also acknowledging that consumers are increasingly demanding authentic, high-excellence products that require reliable labeling systems and designations of origin mechanism. Recommending that hybrid structures, such as cooperatives and consortia, are the most cost-minimizing governance structures for the production, the book highlights that in the case of Italian excellency food, environmental sustainability and economic efficiency are not actually traded off but are reciprocally valorized through the regulation of high-quality standards.

This book will be of great interest to students and scholars of food and wine excellence products, food systems and supply chains, agricultural production and economics and sustainable consumption.

Laura Onofri, MSc (from Catholic University of Leuven, Belgium), PhD (from Maastricht University, the Netherlands) is Research Professor with the Department of Land, Environment, Agriculture and Forestry at the University of Padova, Italy.

Routledge Focus on Environment and Sustainability

Post-Pandemic Sustainable Tourism Management
The New Reality of Managing Ethical and Responsible Tourism
Tony O'Rourke and Marko Koščak

Consumption Corridors
Living a Good Life within Sustainable Limits
Doris Fuchs, Marlyne Sahakian, Tobias Gumbert, Antonietta Di Giulio, Michael Maniates, Sylvia Lorek and Antonia Graf

The Ecological Constitution
Reframing Environmental Law
Lynda Collins

Effective Forms of Environmental Diplomacy
Leila Nicolas and Elie Kallab

Coastal Wetlands Restoration
Public Perception and Community Development
Edited by Hiromi Yamashita

Sustainability in High-Excellence Italian Food and Wine
Laura Onofri

Learning to Live with Climate Change
From Anxiety to Transformation
Blanche Verlie

For more information about this series, please visit: www.routledge.com/Routledge-Focus-on-Environment-and-Sustainability/book-series/RFES

Sustainability in High-Excellence Italian Food and Wine

Laura Onofri

Routledge
Taylor & Francis Group
LONDON AND NEW YORK

earthscan
from Routledge

First published 2022
by Routledge
2 Park Square, Milton Park, Abingdon, Oxon OX14 4RN

and by Routledge
605 Third Avenue, New York, NY 10158

Routledge is an imprint of the Taylor & Francis Group, an informa business

British Library Cataloguing-in-Publication Data
A catalogue record for this book is available from the British Library

Library of Congress Cataloging-in-Publication Data
Names: Onofri, Laura, author.
Title: Sustainability in high-excellence Italian food and wine / Laura Onofri.
Description: New York, NY : Routledge, 2022. | Series: Routledge focus on environment and sustainability | Includes bibliographical references and index.
Identifiers: LCCN 2021013090 (print) | LCCN 2021013091 (ebook) | ISBN 9781032004761 (hardback) | ISBN 9781032004792 (paperback) | ISBN 9781003174325 (ebook)
Subjects: LCSH: Food industry and trade—Italy. | Wine industry—Italy. | Food supply—Italy. | Sustainable agriculture—Italy. | Consumption (Economics)—Environmental aspects—Italy.
Classification: LCC HD9015.I82 O56 2022 (print) | LCC HD9015.I82 (ebook) | DDC 664.0068/4—dc23
LC record available at https://lccn.loc.gov/2021013090
LC ebook record available at https://lccn.loc.gov/2021013091

ISBN: 978-1-032-00476-1 (hbk)
ISBN: 978-1-032-00479-2 (pbk)
ISBN: 978-1-003-17432-5 (ebk)

Typeset in Times New Roman
by Apex CoVantage, LLC

Contents

Illustrations

Figures

Tables

Preface

This text gets inspiration and originates from lecture notes used for courses in *Quality Oriented Food and Wine Management and Governance*, held in the multidisciplinary Italian Food and Wine Master Programme at the University of Padova.

The positive and participatory reaction of graduated students has encouraged me to write an educational book, which can, at the same time, both be enjoyed and understood by all those interested in the subject and represent a simple but rigorous starting point for deepening a current topic.

The excellence of Italian agri-food is now a tautology and a reality of facts spread worldwide. But the excellence of Italian agri-food has various dimensions, sometimes antithetical, which find their synthesis in the sustainable nature of economically efficient production. The book, therefore, examines the reasons for this peculiarity through the qualitative adoption of the theoretical framework and the economics of transaction costs, which is applied to selected case studies, each focusing on a key Italian agri-food product: Parmigiano Reggiano, Mozzarella di Bufala Campana, Amarone wine, Prosecco wine, and Prosciutto di San Daniele. The production and organization of these products face many challenges as they seek to balance competing priorities around economic viability, maintenance of high-quality standards, and environmental and social impacts. The book argues that the development of sustainable and quality models requires changes to the structure and organization of the supply chain while also acknowledging that consumers are increasingly demanding authentic, high-excellence products that require reliable labeling systems and designations of origin mechanism. Recommending that hybrid structures, such as cooperatives and consortia, are the most cost-minimizing governance structures for the production, the book highlights that in the case of Italian excellency food, environmental sustainability, and economic efficiency are not actually traded off but are reciprocally valorized through the regulation of high-quality standards.

This book will be of great interest to students and scholars of food and wine excellence products, food systems and supply chains, agricultural production and economics, and sustainable consumption.

I am very thankful to Andrea Curioni and Edi Defrancesco for inviting me in lecturing in a very stimulating, international Master Programme and to my faculty colleagues, Matteo Marangon *in primis*, for their support and advice. I am grateful to my Master's students for their feedback in the "making". I would like to thank in particular to Marko Sancin, Giorgia Rigon, Aleksei Semenov, Francesco Tatiana Toropygina, and Francesco Fasano. I am thankful to Eleonora Sovrani for graphical support.

In the end, I am very much indebted to Vasco Boatto, a stimulating professor, with a rare mixture of wit intelligence, a sense of humor, and humanity—a real master, to whom I dedicate this work.

1 Introduction

Introduction

Sustainable actions in the agri-food sector are broadly advocated by national and international organizations. Those actions should primarily address a crucial turning point in consumption habits and production methods and technologies. During the 2002 World Summit on Sustainable Development in Johannesburg, for instance, it was emphasized that the change in production and consumption patterns is one of the main preconditions for achieving sustainable development on a global level. The Open Working Group of the United Nations General Assembly (OWG) has proposed 17 Sustainable Development Goals (SDGs) in the 2030 Agenda. Objective no. 12 specifically pursues the challenge of "Guaranteeing sustainable models of production and consumption". In this perspective, Europe has long since embarked on a virtuous path with rules aimed at regulating such an important issue. In July 2008, for instance, the European Commission launched "The Sustainable Consumption and Production and Sustainable Industrial Policy Action", which included a series of proposals for sustainable consumption and production, intending to encourage European industries towards innovation and better environmental policy.[1]

The social and ethical goals of advocated sustainability requirements can be achieved with guaranteed access to food and responsible consumption. In this perspective, to guarantee food safety and safeguard the agri-food sector from recurring crises, the European Union has recently adopted the global intervention strategy "From Farm to Fork" aimed at ensuring a high level of protection of human health and the protection of consumer interests, and by this the effective functioning of the internal market is guaranteed at the same time.

A prerequisite of responsible consumption is the consumer's full awareness of the nutritional value of the food (understood as the absence of contaminants). But it is the guarantee of "quality" (in the broadest sense of the term) that in an increasingly globalized trade context becomes a criticality or strength for the market. Consumers are increasingly becoming careful in considering the intrinsic and extrinsic quality of the products, linked to the production chain and, therefore, to economic, environmental, and social protection in its broadest sense. To promote sustainable and competitive food production, it is, therefore, necessary to develop and promote systemic management at different levels of the agro-ecosystem, aiming at increasing agricultural production and safeguarding natural resources and production inputs at the same time.

On the producers' side, the sustainable use of resources and inputs necessary for food production is a key issue. Modern agriculture, however, has led to a growing specialization of agroecosystems, with a consequent loss of biodiversity and traditional genetic resources, as well as a greater dependence on external factors such as fertilizers, plant protection products, and energy from fossil fuels.[2]

Sustainable economic growth is increasingly becoming a strategic objective of organizations at an international level. In this perspective, producers must adopt and implement strategies based on eco-sustainable management of the agroecosystem.[3] Addressing the challenges of sustainability also means, in harmony with what is proposed by the European Union, focusing on the production and transformation of renewable biological resources and waste into value-added products such as food, feed, bioproducts, and bioenergy through the efficient use of resources and the development of production systems with reduced greenhouse gas emissions, which adapt to and mitigate the negative effects of climate change.[4] It is, therefore, crucial to making the current production and consumption model more efficient by aiming to pursue objectives of sustainability. This means, just to mention a few actions, intervening in the agricultural and industrial sector through the use of environmentally friendly technologies and promoting proper management of resources, a reduction in waste, and an enhancement of waste and waste from the supply chain that favors renewable energy and product development. To do this, it is crucial to intervene in the system with a holistic approach, that addresses both the integration between the various players and the exchange of information in the supply chain.

The quality products of agricultural tradition might be linked to elements of modernity, without changing their identity. Furthermore, considering the role of multifunctional agriculture and referring to the qualitative aspects of the production process in those societies that are more aware and sensible to environmental and cultural dimensions, one should consider accepting an additional price when they comprise factors which nowadays are considered essential.

Quality and sustainability in agri-food markets

The issue of quality and sustainability in agri-food markets is a central theme in the international debate faced by a multiplicity of international organizations, such as FAO or the World Health Organization, and affects trade and the agreements that regulate them. The development of sustainable and quality agri-food sectors requires changes in the structure and organization of supply chains (producer associations, vertical integration, organization of networks) and policies that accompany these processes, ensuring an efficient creation and equity-based distribution of value.

The quality and sustainability of agri-food supply chains aim to contribute to the definition of development trajectories of agricultural and forestry systems that combine the three pillars of sustainable development: (1) economic (development of competitive sectors); (2) social (ensuring the coexistence of different types of subjects, companies, and territories); and (3) environmental. Sustainability is defined as a three-pillar equilibrium, based on social, economic, and environmental sustainability requirements. (UN, 2015). In this perspective, the challenging task is finding the equilibrium between forces and dynamics that often produce a trade-off.[5]

On the other hand, consumers increasingly demand authentic products obtained with specific and traditional methods. Reliable labeling systems and designations of origin are some of the tools used to communicate product characteristics and production methods to buyers and consumers. A system of effective rules, controls, and sanctions is needed to protect consumers and producers from unsustainable and low-quality product trading practices, with particular attention to public regulation and voluntary certification systems including organic farming or the standards required by producers. Moreover, the pursuit of quality can represent an important antidote against the dangers of product homologation.

In this context, it is crucial to define the boundaries of quality in the agri-food sector. The concept of "quality" in the production of food is complex, and for this reason, it might be often misused. There are many possible meanings of "quality" in the agri-food system. This concept of quality is becoming a global, multidimensional paradigm that can be analyzed from different perspectives and many points of view since it incorporates objective and subjective components. Global quality includes tangible and intangible factors and concerns both product and production process.

A preliminary distinction must be made between (1) product quality, referring to particular qualitative characteristics that differentiate a product from another of the same category and (2) system quality, referring in general to the ability of the producer, processor, distributor, or retailer to produce foods with characteristics that meet customer expectations over time.

Both concepts, however, implicitly presuppose that the hygienic integrity of the food in question is ensured. In other words, when it comes to product or system quality in a food company, it is assumed that the food or food products produced by the company itself cannot harm human health. Otherwise, it would not be lawful to associate the term "food" with the product.

Several factors affect and determine the total quality of agri-food products, and processes are in place to identify selected ones: (1) hygienic/sanitary quality,[6] (2) chemical nutritional quality,[7] (3) legal quality,[8] (4) organoleptic quality,[9] and (5) quality of origin.[10]

In the end the quality of agri-food products is often guaranteed by a certification (product or system) mechanism issued by independent third parties and strictly connected to the quality concepts listed earlier. In this perspective, it is possible to distinguish between (1) product certification and (2) system certification. Product certifications guarantee that each product sold and marketed by a firm complies with specific requirements expressly stated. In any case, certified products must possess specific characteristics as compared to products of the same kind. In turn, these certifications can be divided into (1) regulated certifications that are governed by legislative provisions (generally of European derivation), typical examples of which are the PDO, PGI, TSG certifications, linked to the territorial origin, and the organic certifications, linked to the methods of cultivation, breeding, the transformation of primary materials; (2) unregulated certifications that are based on specifications containing product requirements, specially prepared by the firm. System certifications guarantee that the firm can meet the customer's expectations by ensuring that the qualitative characteristics of the product (which do not necessarily have to be higher or different than those of similar products) are those that are declared.

From quality to excellency in the Italian food and wine sector

A high-quality reputation is increasingly becoming necessary to support the competitiveness and profitability of the agriculture and agri-food sectors, in particular, of the Italian one which, not being able to count on large economies of scale, has always focused on the excellence of its products. Over the years, the agri-food production sector has become one of the most important economic activities of "*Made in Italy*" brand. In 2019, the Italian food industry was confirmed, with a turnover of 140 billion euros and 54,400 companies and around 8% of national GDP, as the second sector of national manufacturing after mechanics, ranking third in Europe, and close to the German and French food industry. The current challenge for the Italian food industry lies in the ability to look further to enter new markets, as well as defending and expanding the consolidated ones, aiming to conquer European leadership with a view to retain greater sustainability.

In this perspective, the high quality of Italian agri-food becomes "excellent" for some products associated with the "concept of *Made in Italy*" in national and international markets. *Made in Italy* is one of the most known and appreciated brands in the world, the trademark of the know-how that distinguishes Italy in the eyes of other countries. Creativity, quality, and Italian lifestyle are expressed mainly in the areas of clothing, furniture, mechanical automation, and agri-food. But the world itself has changed over the years, and "*Made in Italy*" has increasingly needed precise definitions, legal protections, and rules as a shelter from counterfeits, scams, unfair competition, and from false or misleading indications of origin that mislead consumers.[11]

The boundaries depend on the sector in question and are identified by legislation that includes various texts. Agri-food excellence incorporates the concept of *Made in Italy* and attributes, a plethora of characteristics inextricably linked to "lifestyle, beauty, monuments, culture, and undoubtedly to food" to the product, in addition to quality tout court. In particular, some agri-food products, such as Parmigiano Reggiano or Amarone della Valpolicella wine, are iconic representations of *Made in Italy*. This aspect has been extensively explored under various dimensions, especially under those of communication and marketing to support entry and hold in new markets.

The iconic perspective of high Italian food excellence is scrutinized in this book from the point of view of sustainability and the sustainable dimension of the production of these products. Through the pursuit of excellence and quality, sustainability is achieved, and, conversely, the pursuit and implementation of sustainability reinforce excellence.

The book demonstrates that to gain excellency in Italian food, economic and environmental sustainability do not trade-off and self-enforce each other by adding a high value to the product. Five iconic products of *Made in Italy* agri-food excellence are selected for five case studies.

These products (Parmigiano Reggiano, Amarone della Valpolicella, Mozzarella di Bufala Campana, Prosecco, and Prosciutto di San Daniele del Friuli) are characterized by production practices that, although innovative and advanced in technology, retain millenary expertise, a capital of traditional knowledge accumulated from a millenary tradition. Parmigiano Reggiano, for example, was born in the Middle Ages from the need of the monks to produce a cheese that could be preserved for a long time. Amarone wine originates from the ancient Roman tradition of wine and is mentioned by the Latin chroniclers.

From this point of view, the excellence of the selected products depends on the dynamics that include, in the making, economic, social, and environmental sustainability.

In this perspective, the book's main thesis is the preliminary assumption that high-excellence Italian food and wine producers are profit maximizers. However, the profit maximization objective in the case of the selected high excellence agri-food products (and for all Italian high excellency agri-food products) is implemented through a production and governance organization that results in making, in turn, economically efficient, technologically innovative, and sustainability-oriented products.

Main thesis and organization of the book

The book is organized as follows. The first chapter illustrates the main thesis and "sets the scene". It provides the book motivation and illustrates the adopted methodological approach. It addresses and discusses two main topics.

The first topic is a qualitative, nontechnical but rigorous introduction of the foundations of economic theory and explains why this discipline is useful to address the treated topics. In this perspective, the contribution aims to provide the reader with the foundations of economic thinking for carrying on an independent analysis. In particular, the chapter defines the discipline and an illustration and explanation of the main concepts that are needed to think and analyze in an economic perspective (scarcity, trade-offs, marginalism, (opportunity) costs and benefits, market equilibrium including market demand and supply formation, market failures, externalities, with a focus on environmental externalities and sustainability, among the others). The chapter also offers a synthesis of the analytical toolbox required to perform economic analysis. The reason why economists need to use mathematical, graphical, and statistical analysis is presented, as well as why and how those tools are useful to address the main topics of the book.

In particular, the book adopts the analytical framework provided by transaction costs economics (TCE). According to TCE, the most efficient governance structure associated with industrial production, including agri-food, is the one resulting from efficient transaction costs (TC) minimization. Transaction costs are the costs of running the economic system of firms (Williamson, 1979). The theory suggests that each type of transaction produces coordination costs of monitoring, controlling, and managing transactions. They mostly depend on three key variables: (1) uncertainty of the transaction, (2) complexity of the transaction, and (3) asset specificity required by the transaction. The degree of intensity of such variables affects the level (quantitatively or qualitatively quantified) of the transaction costs, which, in turn, define the most efficient governance structure.[12] The economic background is fundamental to understanding and analyzing, in a qualitative, nontechnical perspective, the question of why agri-food firms invest in quality since quality differentiation presents costs and benefits that are thoroughly discussed and presented. Another question relates to studying how quality-oriented agri-food firms organize the production and commercialization of their products. From such a perspective, an emphasis is placed on the economics of organization through the adoption of the TCE approach, and it is shown how agri-food consortia are efficient transaction costs minimizing governance structure for the organization of quality-based Italian food and wine markets. The second topic focuses on sustainability as a key factor for food quality and security. It explains and describes how environmental sustainability impacts production and consumption choices of selected quality Italian food and wine and how sustainability in quality food markets has (positively) affected the market equilibria and performance and the market organization and governance. For instance, this may occur through a careful selection of (most costly) but highly sustainable production inputs, with criteria and protocols that are indicated in the firms' consortia statutes and regulations and with a careful certification strategy.

In the end, the book presents a collection of case studies that show how the Italian agri-food sector, producing high excellence outputs, is reorganizing to face sustainability challenges and keep high-quality levels. For instance, Parmigiano Reggiano, Mozzarella di Bufala Campana, Prosciutto di San Daniele, Amarone wine, and Prosecco wine, among the others, are well-known examples of excellence in Italian food and wine sector. The products were selected based on different criteria. On the one hand, an attempt has been made to include products such as Parmigiano Reggiano which are very popular and well known. On the other hand, products such as Buffalo Mozzarella from Campania have been chosen, which not only represent agri-food excellence, but also are an attempt to counter clichés and beliefs in difficult social contexts. All products are the result of ancient tradition and millenary knowledge.

The selected case studies are analyzed in light of the theoretical and economic background and framework presented in the first part of the book. The production and organization of those outputs need to address and solve the challenge generated by the potential trade-off between technological efficiency, cost minimization, maintenance of high-quality standards, transaction cost minimization structures and governance, reputation, and environmental sustainability, requiring a thorough revision and re-conceptualization on the use of production inputs, the organization of production, certification, just to mention a few.

The selection also attempts to focus on high-excellence food and wines, whose production is distributed across the Italian territory, as shown in Figure 1.1.

Figure 1.1 Geographical Distribution of Selected Products

For each excellency product, the related chapter provides: (1) a description of the product, market characteristics, and performance. In this perspective, row quantitative information and selected market and market performance indicators are computed with available data (annual production, annual revenues and profits, commercialization, annual demand, use of selected inputs, amount of used production inputs, price index, and so on); (2) a description of sustainable production practices and the indicators; and (3) the application of TCE analysis to the product and market at stake.

The case studies are also key examples to show how markets have re-adapted and reorganized, even recovering and valorizing traditional knowledge and expertise to embody sustainability requirements in food quality and safety. The case studies are stand-alone chapters and are organized following the same structural architecture.

In synthesis, profit maximizer producers aim at organizing the production efficiently. From a TCE perspective, they are efficient in minimizing transaction costs and in organizing production under the most efficient, transaction costs minimizing governance structure. It turns out that in all cases, the most efficient TC-minimizing governance structure is the consortium hybrid governance, which secures a triple objective: (1) profit maximization, (2) organization of production under an optimal governance structure, and (3) sustainability, interpreted as high quality of the product, social cohesion, value creation, and being environment friendly.

Notes

1 Italy immediately implemented this indication with the document drawn up by the Ministry of the Environment. In this context, the World Health Organization recently published the European Food and Nutrition Action Plan 2015–2020, helping to outline the governance of the food system for a higher quality of food and well-being deriving from balanced diets.

2 In addition to previous problems (such as erosion, drought, compaction, salinization, chemical pollution of the soil and water, the loss of organic matter, and the imbalance of nutrients), agriculture must also deal with the new criticalities caused by the rapid alteration of the biogeochemical cycles of some greenhouse gases by the extinction of species and by the emergence of new parasites and pathogens. All these problems contribute heavily to the imbalance of the agro-ecosystem with repercussions on the entire supply chain. Since an increase in cultivated areas worldwide or an increase in the quantity of water for irrigation cannot be pursued, the recovery of soils and anthropized agricultural areas, therefore, becomes a necessity

3 These include i) the protection of microbial biodiversity, ii) the reduction of the content of chemical and microbiological contaminants from primary production, iii) the development and use of targeted agronomic practices, iv) the enhancement and conservation of local and resilient resources, v) the use of prevention and control models of phytopathogens, and vi) the use of "precision farming" techniques and forecasting models aimed at reducing the use of chemicals and, where possible, replacing synthetic active ingredients with molecules of natural origin with antimicrobial action. It is also necessary to develop systems to intervene in process technologies for the abatement of toxic residues in food and feed and at the same time for the reduction of the use of preservatives; to use innovative packaging capable of preventing microbiological risk, effectively control the degradation of products and favor the extension of the shelf life, and adopt technologies in the production, conservation, and storage phases; and to allow great benefits in terms of guaranteeing safety, traceability, control, and reduction of degradation and contamination phenomena.

4 In this perspective, R&D activities must allow the production system to position itself "one step ahead" of the regulatory requirements, providing the control system with adequate analytical tools and, for consumers, scientific evidence to make informed consumption choices and adopt correct food-use practices. The use of integrated platforms that are able to manage, integrate, and make data and information available along the supply chains can allow the production system to make a great progress. Accompanying products with data and information collected along the production chain can allow the traceability of production batches and guarantee the traceability of raw materials.

5 The concept of sustainability is discussed in Chapter 2.

6 The hygienic-sanitary quality of food is guaranteed by a compliance with minimum hygiene requirements, established by law, relating to the "content" of

microorganisms and their metabolic (toxins) in chemical substances. According to EU (2004), "food hygiene" means the measures and conditions necessary to control the dangers and ensure the suitability of a food product for human consumption, taking into account its intended use.

Chemical residues present in food can derive from a primary contamination, that is, an upstream of the production process, due to the presence of pesticide residues (normally used in agriculture), the presence of heavy metals (especially for crops placed along the roads), and the excessive use of drugs on-farm made even more serious by non-compliance with the suspension times provided for by law; chemical residues present in food can derive from a secondary contamination too, which can occur during the transport, storage, or sale of food products if normal hygiene rules are not followed.

The presence of microorganisms inside the food, in addition to causing alterations such as putrefaction, rancidity, fermentation of sugars, with a consequent variation of the organoleptic characteristics, can also cause the following: i) food poisoning: following the consumption of foods containing toxins produced by microorganisms that have multiplied in the food before its consumption, therefore, the microorganism can also be dead or even absent, the one that determines the intoxication is the toxin produced by it; ii) food infections: following the consumption of food containing live microorganisms, which has reached the intestine, microorganisms multiply causing the infection; iii) food poisoning: they occur following the consumption of foods containing live microorganisms and their toxins.

7 The chemical/nutritional quality of food is given by its content in proteins, lipids, and carbohydrates and is, therefore, the nutritional capacity of the food itself.

The nutritional quality of food can be understood under:

- the quantitative aspect, which is given by the amount of chemical energy it provides; and
- the qualitative aspect, which is given by the combination of the nutritional elements it contains.

The nutritional quality of food must be guaranteed at every level of the production process, starting with the choice of raw materials; some treatments, then, can influence the content of nutritional elements of food; for example, heat denatures proteins, with consequent loss of the biological properties of the same; a correct storage/distribution process also plays a fundamental role in guaranteeing the chemical/nutritional quality of food.

8 Legal quality is guaranteed by a set of rules affecting the food sector: to be defined as conforming to the quality, a food product must meet certain minimum legal requirements.

The Italian legislation protects the health of a citizen with a large number of laws. Alongside the legislation that encompasses the entire food sector, there are more specific legislations concerning particular food sectors and even more specific ones concerning particular food products within that sector. The cheese sector, for example, is regulated by a large number of laws; that is, the production of Parmigiano Reggiano, or Pecorino Romano, or Mozzarella di Bufala Campana, to name a few, is governed by a series of regulations that refer to these products.

9 The organoleptic quality of food is given by a consumer's evaluation of certain characteristics of the food itself, such as appearance, aroma, and texture,

perceived through the sense organs (sensory quality). These are therefore subjective consumer assessments, which are significantly influenced by psychological, social, and cultural factors.

With sight, the food is evaluated for its color, shape, size, and also for the way it is presented. Sight is, among the five senses, the one that most influences the choice of food and that in turn conditions the other sense organs. The smell in general and the smell of a food product are perceived, which can be pleasant or unpleasant. The texture in general or texture (compactness, hardness, density, etc.) of a food product, and, in the case of fresh foods, the state of conservation and/or maturation is perceived by touch.

The bitterness, saltiness, sweetness, and acidity of food are perceived with the taste.

With the hearing sense, particular characteristics are perceived that can indicate the freshness, through the noise associated with chewing of some food products (biscuits, cereals, etc.).

10 In 1992, the European Community created some systems known as PDO (Protected Designation of Origin), PGI (Protected Geographical Indication), and TSG (Traditional Specialty Guaranteed) to promote and protect agro-food products. The PDO and PGI mark further protect the consumer, guaranteeing that "An agricultural or food product that benefits from one of the aforementioned types of reference should satisfy certain conditions listed in a specification" (art. 10, EU, 2006).

11 In general, it is possible to insert the "Made in Italy" mark of origin if the product is entirely made in Italy or if it has undergone the last substantial transformation in Italy. The trademark provided for by law 350/2009 links it to the selection criterion of the Community Customs Code of 1992 and that introduced by Legislative Decree 135/2009 (Article 6, paragraph 1) which deals with the so-called "full Made in Italy".

Law 350/2003 (finance law 2004, art.4, paragraph 49) specified that "the stamp" made in Italy "on products and goods not originating in Italy according to the European legislation on origin constitutes a false indication". The rule, therefore, referred to the Community Customs Code EC 2913/1992 (articles 23–24), according to which "a commodity to whose production two or more countries have contributed originates from the country where the last substantial transformation or processing took place, economically justified and carried out in an undertaking equipped for this purpose, which resulted in the manufacture of a new product or which represented an important stage in the manufacturing process".

This was then replaced by the new updated Code (EC Regulation 450/2008), which governs two principles in a single article (36): "Goods wholly obtained in a single country or territory are considered to originate in that country or territory. Goods to the production of which two or more countries or territories have contributed are considered to originate in the country or territory where they underwent the last substantial transformation". Here the reference is made to non-preferential (customs) origin: regardless of the percentages of domestic or foreign goods used in production. The indication of the mark of origin is therefore not granted if the transformation activity is not carried out in Italy or if—even carried out in our country—it is however marginal. False or misleading indications of origin or origin are punished under Article 517 of the Penal Code.

12 Williamson (1979) shows that asset specificity increases the uncertainty and complexity of the transaction and therefore transaction costs. The higher asset

specificity, the higher the uncertainty and complexity of the transactions, the lower the reliance on the (neoclassical) market mechanism (that does not guarantee the minimization of transaction costs), and the higher the reliance on long-term contracts or other complex institutional structures.

References

EU (2004). Regulation (EC) No 852/2004 of the European Parliament and of the Council of 29 April 2004 on the Hygiene of Foodstuffs.

EU (2006). Council Regulation (EC) No 510/2006 of 20 March 2006 on the Protection of Geographical Indications and Designations of Origin for Agricultural Products and Foodstuffs.

UN (2015). *Transforming Our World: The 2030 Agenda for Sustainable Development*. UN General Assembly, 21 October (A/RES/70/1).

Williamson, O. (1979). Transaction-Cost Economics: The Governance of Contractual Relations. *Journal of Law and Economics*, 22, 233–261.

Part I
Background

2 Economic thinking and methodological analytical toolbox

1. Introduction

The chapter introduces, in a nontechnical but rigorous way, the foundations of economic theory and explains why this discipline is useful to address the treated topics. The chapter aims to provide the reader with the main foundations of economic thinking for understanding the book architecture and case-study chapters and for carrying on independent analysis. In particular, the chapter defines the discipline's main content and features and provides explanations of the main concepts that are needed to think and analyze from an economic perspective. These include the concepts of scarcity, trade-offs, marginality (opportunity) costs and benefits, market equilibrium including market demand and supply formation, perfect competition market failures, externalities, with a focus on environmental externalities, sustainability, among others. The chapter also offers a synthesis of the analytical toolbox, required to perform economic analysis. The reasons why economists need to use mathematical, graphical, and statistical analysis are presented as well as why and how those tools are useful to perform (qualitative) economic analysis. In the end, the chapter provides the main foundations of TCE, which is the adopted branch of economic theory for the analysis of the case studies.

2. Economic thinking and methodology

Economics is "the science of choices in a context of scarce resources" (L. Robbins, 1932). The understanding of human choices in contexts of scarce resources and the valuation and management of scarcity are at the very heart of economic science. Besides, the concept of a resource is a relative and dynamic concept, with a role and value that vary over time and space, depending on social organization, ability to use as per the resource availability, quality, and cultural and ethical value. The "paradox of water and diamond", which goes back to Adam Smith and the Marginalists, however, represents an emblematic synthesis and example of value determination in a scarcity context. Water is a vital resource, particularly useful, but has low value in the markets. Diamonds are extremely valuable in the market but not particularly useful. The key difference in the way value is attached to such emblematic resources lies in the different availability of the resources. Diamonds are scarcer than water.

Scarcity implies that human choice is constrained. When dealing with scarcity, homo economicus (the economic agent), selfish and rational by theoretical construction, aims at achieving his objectives and pursue his self-interest. However, limited resources imply that the full realization of objectives is not possible since scarcity generates constraints and limited achievements of the objectives that determine the choice.

In this perspective, constrained choice in a context of scarcity also implies confronting and valuing what is given up with what is selected, since resources are not infinite, and every choice implies a trade-off. Economic agents, therefore, have to think in terms of alternatives. The consequence of thinking in terms of alternatives and trade-offs is the requirement to define a choice criterion. Such criterion is essentially based on the evaluation (from qualitative to quantitative, including monetary terms) of costs and benefits of (individual and social) choices. Costs are broadly defined as the disadvantages generated by giving up. Benefits are the advantage that is derived from the choice. In solving the trade-off between desired options and constraints (determined by the scarcity of the resource), the economic agent values the margin. Economics implies thinking of the constrained choice on the "margin". Economists look at "small" variations in trade-offs, since dealing with scarcity requires focusing on small variations from the starting equilibrium. A trivial but effective example is the situation where one deals with a short blanket that cannot cover both feet and shoulders. This implies a trade-off that is not always solved in a dichotomous fashion: either feet or shoulders. Most often, the person will attempt to adapt to the scarcity constraint by modulating on the margin the use of an item. It is not the total or average value that determines the value, for example, of production input but rather its incremental value (which can later be "scaled up" to define the total value). The economic value of a resource is measured on the margin.

In Simon's definition, economics is a science; therefore, it is based on scientific methods like mathematics, statistics, and econometrics. Economists use models to simplify reality to improve the understanding of the world. The scientific method acknowledges the use of different assumptions to address different problems (related to performing choices in a world of scarce resources). Economists make assumptions to make the world easier to understand. The main difficulty in scientific thinking is deciding which assumptions to make. This is also based on examining and understanding how certain events and contingencies are related. This implies finding a (theoretical) nexus of cause and effect between assumptions and deriving theoretical predictions that are empirically tested through data analysis. The models embody the main dimension of economic thinking. They usually contain one (or more) objective functions that embody the (representative) economic agents' objective function and the mathematical constraint. In a world of scarce resources, the achievement of purposes through choice is always constrained. This is mathematically translated with the adoption of constrained maximization models. This also embodies the concept of trade-off. The solution of those models is the equilibrium solution that is determined, on the margin, by differential calculus, capturing the small variations.

Solving for the constrained maximization problems is not a theoretical, mathematical exercise per se. In the economic frameworks, this is applied in the contexts of "human choice". Mostly, "human choice" refers to production and consumption choices, even if the economic thinking and methods have been applied to a plethora of different contexts. In a simplified, schematized scenario, the representative consumer aims to choose what to consume within a set of goods and services and in what quantities. The representative consumer derives pleasure from consumption. However, resources are scarce, and he cannot afford all goods and services he would like to consume. Transforming such an economic dimension of choice in mathematical modeling implies defining a consumer objective function (the utility function that maps consumers' preferences for goods and services) that is maximized in a constrained setting that forces trade-offs. The constraint is represented by the consumers' available budget line. The solution to such an economic–mathematical problem will define the number of goods and services that the consumer prefers and can afford at a given price schedule.

Similarly, the representative producer aims at "making money" for production and sales activities. However, and again, the amount of output that the producer can make is limited by the available technological production processes and by the available resources and production factors. In this scenario, transforming the economic dimension of choice in mathematical modeling implies defining a producer objective function (the profit function that relates producers' revenues and costs) that is maximized in a constrained setting that forces trade-offs. The constraint is represented by the available production technology, expressed by a production function. The solution to such an economic–mathematical problem will define the number of goods and services that the producers can make and can afford at given price schedules. The representative consumer and producer, by assumption, synthesize the behavior of many consumers and producers that choose along the same line and criteria. The total number of consumers who want to purchase a particular good or service represents the demand for that good or service. Similarly, the total number of producers who want to sell a particular good or service represents the supply of the good and service. Supply and demand represent the "two sides" of the same problem: choosing in a world of scarce resources. The implementation of producers' and consumers' choices occurs in markets. Markets can be defined as "institutions" where demand and supply meet, and exchange occurs at the market-clearing price. In this context, the price is the most efficient signal of scarcity, equilibrium, and social welfare, since it conveys information on the "true" value of all resources. Such theoretical construction implies that markets allow economic agents to pursue their (consumption and production) goals. By pursuing individual objectives (deriving pleasure from consumption/making profits), consumers and producers, driven by an "invisible hand", satisfy their needs and implement their choice in the markets. In this perspective, markets are those institutions where economic agents can achieve their needs. Besides, when markets are in perfect competition, scarce resources are allocated in the best possible way (i.e., they are used efficiently). These two features allow the achievement of the maximization of social welfare.

To implement all possible benefits derived from the exchange, markets' structure has to be characterized by perfect competition. This implies that there are no barriers to entry into the market, and all consumers who want to purchase and producers who want to sell can do so. In this setting, the number of producers and consumers is large, so that no participant in the exchange has the bargaining power to "make" the price. The equilibrium price is determined by the exchange dynamics and is observed and "taken" by economic agents participating in the market exchange. The perfect competition also implies perfect information and knowledge of all parties about the exchange conditions. When the perfect competition conditions do not hold, markets fail to achieve all the benefits derived from the exchange. In this case, the price mechanism is not able to signal the "true" (shadow) value of resources, because there might be dynamics that are "external" to the price formation and are not embodied in the value signaled by the price, like in the case of externalities (Mankiew, 2001).[1]

Besides, when the market fails resources are not allocated in the best (efficient) way for social welfare. Moreover, a quota of producers and consumers who want to participate in the exchange is left out because the price is higher and the supplied quantity smaller than the combination price–quantity under perfect competition. This is the case of market structures characterized by monopoly and oligopoly, where producers are not price takers but are able, under defined conditions, to "make" the price and appropriate exchange surplus (Mankiew, 2001).[2] On the contrary, a quota of consumers might benefit from the consumption of particular goods, like public goods, without paying and free-riding on other consumers who pay for the good (Mankiew, 2001).[3]

When the market fails, the policymaker intervenes by designing and implementing regulatory measures, aiming at correcting the failure and revamping perfect competition conditions.

3. Transaction costs economics

The previous section has synthetically sketched the main concepts and definitions of economic thinking and theory. Economics, however, is a complex science, characterized by a plethora of methods and different branches, streams of thought, and specializations. The previous section has summarized the main features and commonalities across different approaches. TCE represents an important branch of economic theory. The main foundations of TCE are conceptualized by Ronald Coase and Oliver Williamson, both Nobel Prize winners in Economic Sciences. TCE addresses the theory of exchange in a more "concrete" and realistic way. The starting point is Ronald Coase's seminal paper, "The Theory of the Firm" (*Economica*, 1937), where the author develops a theory that explains why firms exist and why some transactions are carried on in markets and others are performed inside the firm. Oliver Williamson discusses and explains Coase's starting point in detail by explaining why transactions are carried on in institutions different than markets and firms and by enriching the theory with the definition of a model architecture that includes behavioral assumptions and key explanatory variables.

In the "general" neoclassic economic thinking perspective, TCE is also based on the trading-off of costs and benefits derived from choice. In particular, TCE theorizes that the way exchanges are organized depends on the costs and the benefits deriving from the transaction itself. TCE explains the existence of different governance structures that are the result of the attempt to maximize the benefits from the exchange and balancing/minimizing the costs of the exchange. Transaction cost economics focuses on alternative modes of organizing transactions (and/or governance structures) that minimize transaction costs (Williamson, 1979, 1986). From the TCE perspective, the optimum organizational structure is the one that achieves economic efficiency by minimizing the costs of exchange. The theory suggests that each type of transaction produces TC. TC is the costs of organizing the transaction and, in general, refers to the costs of negotiating, monitoring, and governing exchanges among economic agents. They are generated by the exchange and are the preparatory costs of search and information, preliminary to the transaction. They are the bargaining and decision costs, borne during the exchange. They also are the monitoring, policing, and enforcement costs generated by activities posterior to the exchange. In particular, Williamson has defined TC broadly as the costs of running the economic system of firms. TC must be distinguished from production costs. A decision-maker can choose to use different governance structures (for instance spot markets or vertical integration) by comparing transaction costs with internal production costs. Thus, the cost is the primary determinant of such a decision.

The TCE conceptual background prescribes for a particular behavioral setting. The neoclassical assumptions of economic agents' behavior are refined in a more realistic perspective. In particular, in the TCE setting, economic agents have a bounded rationality. Like in the neoclassical frame, economic agents have the knowledge and the methods to rank their preferences and rationally make choices accordingly; however, that rationality is bounded by the impossibility to know every possible contingency in every possible moment of the exchange. This hampers the possibility to perfectly predict the outcome and consequences, probabilistically generated by the occurrence of unexpected, unforecastable (given bounded rationality) events. This implies that it may be too costly, if not impossible, to consider all consequences of a decision (or an exchange).

Besides, TCE reframes the neoclassical condition of self-interest (economic agents maximize their welfare) by specifying a behavioral frame where self-interest is characterized by guile. That is, in a TCE framework, economic agents behave opportunistically. This implies that some agents will behave differently from what they appear to be doing.

Bounded rationality and opportunistic behavior represent the behavioral necessary and sufficient conditions that generate transaction costs. The magnitude and degree of the TC, on the other end, depend on three different variables: (1) asset specificity, (2) uncertainty, and (3) complexity of the transaction. The degree of intensity of such variables affects the level (quantitatively or qualitatively quantified) of the transaction costs.

Asset specificity is a measure of the degree to which a productive asset is committed to a specific task and cannot be redeployed to alternative uses without incurring high (opportunity) costs, that is without sacrificing the majority of its productive value. Asset specificity can be quantified as the quota of investment value to the transaction or exchange that is lost when the asset is used outside the specific exchange setting or transaction relationship. There are different asset specificities. It is worth mentioning the most important. Site specificity refers to the geographical location of an asset that impacts the economic use of the asset if it is restricted to a particular area, and the accessibility or the distance can increase costs and time of the exchange. Physical asset specificity refers to machinery, technologies, or other physical production factors, like warehouses of buildings, which have narrowly defined use. Human asset specificity is the particular skill or training that applies only to the specialized area under exchange. Dedicated assets are investments specifically required by one or more of the contracting parties for the sake and purpose of the transaction at stake. Brand name capital specificity implies the affiliation with a well-known brand name, making the affiliated party less free to pursue different opportunities. Temporal asset specificity is linked to assets where the coordination of exchange activities and/or the organization of the transaction are strictly characterized by particular timing and/or procedural steps that must follow strict timing requirements.

Uncertainty is the variable capturing the probabilistic dimension of the transaction realization. Primary uncertainty is generated by exogenous events such as natural events like climate change, and expected/unexpected variations in demand (i.e., consumers' preferences) and supply (i.e., technology of production) as well as in regulation. Behavioral uncertainty refers to endogenous events, generated by the transaction parties and the contracting choices and setting (i.e., lack of trust).

Complexity refers to the degree of sophistication of the exchange/ transaction. It increases, among other factors, with the frequency (low, medium, high) of the transaction; the completeness/incompleteness of the contract; and the number of parties and activities involved to prepare, implement, and monitor the exchange.

The behavioral characteristics of the transaction/exchange (bounded rationality and opportunistic behavior) generate transaction costs. They increase the cost of organizing, implementing, and monitoring the exchange. The magnitude and degree of the transaction costs depend on the existence (and related magnitude) of assets' specificity, uncertainty, and complexity. The existence, degree, and magnitude of the transaction costs affect, in turn, the choice of the governance structure adopted for performing the transaction in transaction-costs-minimizing way that allows maximizing the surplus (benefit) generated by the exchange itself. Production organization and exchange are more complex in reality than neoclassical theory, and TCE attempts to address and embody such complexity in the model architecture. The reasoning is summarized in Figure 2.1.

Transaction costs minimizing governance structures vary, according to the degree and magnitude of TC. They can span from spot markets, on one extreme when TC are negligible, to "hierarchy", that is fully vertically integrated structures, where all productive activities and exchanges occur within one or more firms or organizations, on the other extreme, when TC

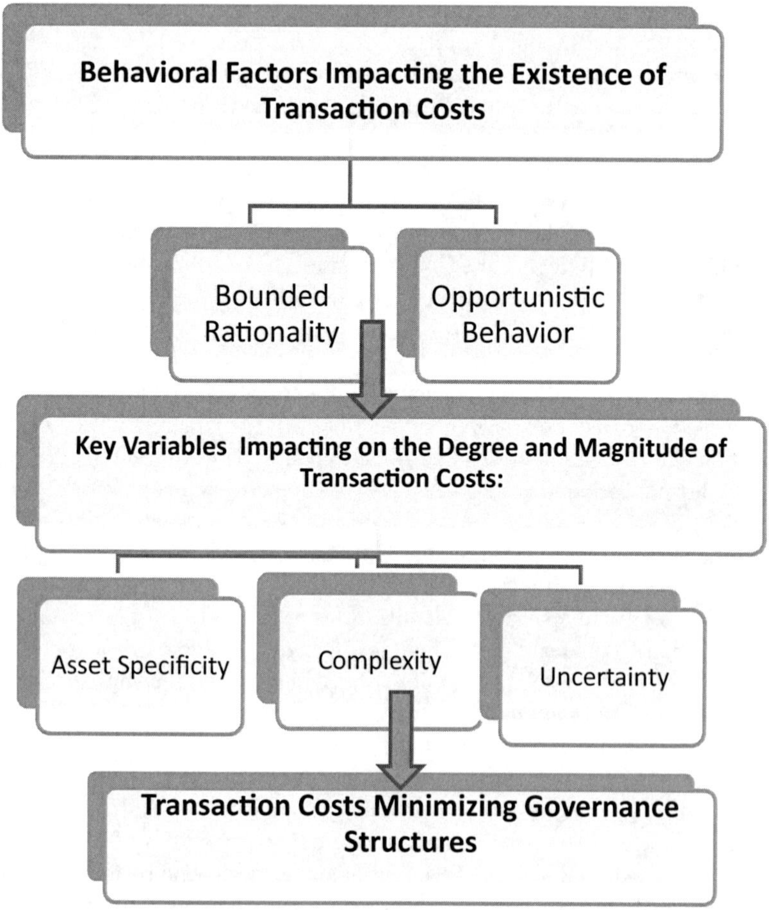

Figure 2.1 TCE Model Architecture

are extremely high. Between the two extremes, a plethora of "hybrid" governance structures[4] (contracts, franchising, cooperatives, cartels, consortia, joint ventures, just to mention a few) exist. In this framework, markets, "hybrids", and firms are alternative instruments for completing a related set of transactions. The relative efficiency (measured in terms of TC minimization) determines which mode is adopted. In particular, firms exist because it is difficult to use the price system to coordinate all economic activities. The question always is if it pays to bring an extra exchange transaction under the organizing authority. There are "costs of using the price mechanism" (Coase, 1937, p. 3), and the more complex the transaction the higher the

Table 2.1 Governance Structures and TC

		Degree of Uncertainty		Degree of Complexity as Frequency of Transactions	
		Low	**High**	**Low**	**High**
Degree of Asset Specificity	Low	Market	Market	Market	Hybrid
	High	Hybrid	Hybrid	Market	Hierarchy/vertical integration

Source: Adapted from Williamson (1979)

price of the market. At the margin, the costs of organizing within the firm will be equal either to the costs of organizing in another firm or to the costs involved in leaving to the transaction to be "organized" by the price mechanism. (Coase, 1937).

Table 2.1 reports selected examples where (selected) governance structures are a function of asset specificity and the degree of uncertainty and complexity (expressed as transaction frequencies).

Markets, hybrids, and firms represent alternative instruments for completing transactions. There are situations where the firm produces inputs inside or buys outside. The first case is not explained by neoclassical theory. In this perspective, the higher asset specificity, the higher the uncertainty and complexity of the transactions, the lower the reliance on the (neoclassical) market mechanism (that does not guarantee the minimization of transaction costs), and the higher the reliance on long-term contracts or another complex, hierarchical institutional structure, like vertical integration. On the contrary, when the degree of asset specificity, uncertainty, and complexity is low, markets are the most TC-minimizing governance structure, since the transaction at stake does not require complex coordination to manage the TC. There are "intermediate" situations when the degree of asset specificity is high, and the degree of uncertainty is low. In this case, the specific investment required to perform the transaction is not easily redeployed, and this increases TC. However, if the degree of uncertainty is relatively low, the most efficient governance structure is represented by a "hybrid" structure, like, for instance, a long-term contract (LTC). Such instrument differs from a "one-shot", spot market contract, where asset-specific investment might not be remunerated on the margin and requires a certain degree of reliance and time duration but has a more flexible (and less costly) structure than vertical integration.

4. Conceptual framework

The section provides a simple model that represents the conceptual framework and methodological apparatus for the analysis and the testing of the selected case studies, presented in the second part of the book. The model incorporates and summarizes the contents described in the previous parts of the chapter. The model is designed based on the thesis that the structure adopted to govern transactions for the selected products (Parmigiano Reggiano, Mozzarella di Bufala Campana; Prosecco and Amarone wines and Prosciutto di San Daniele) is the most TC minimizing. Such structure allows to efficiently manage TC, preserve excellence, and pursue sustainability. Equation (1) describes the model.

$$\textit{TC minimizing Governance Structure} = \min(\textit{TC}\,(\textit{uncertainty}\,(\bullet), \textit{complexity}\,(\bullet), \textit{asset specificity}\,(\bullet), \alpha)) \quad (1)$$

The TC-minimizing Governance Structure (markets, hybrid, or vertical integration) is the dependent variable that is determined by the degree and magnitude of transaction costs (TC) generated by the organization of transactions for the selected products. Transaction costs, in turn, depend on the three key variables: uncertainty, complexity, and asset specificity, The three variables, in turn, are affected by a set of variables (·) that are identified on a case-by-case basis. The three key variables affect TC mostly because of the high qualitative level required to organize and coordinate the output production and exchange.

Besides, the TC-minimizing governance structure also depends on the parameter α that represents the degree of sustainability that affects the amount and magnitude of TC. Incorporating sustainability in the production and transaction of the selected goods might affect the degree and magnitude of transaction costs and, in turn, contribute to determine the TC-minimizing governance structure.

In our framework, we adopt the definition of sustainability provided by the United Nations (UN).[5] According to the resolution adopted by the general assembly on 27 July 2012 (UN, 2012a), the concept of sustainability refers to three "pillars" that make the development of economic activities and the protection of the environment compatible:

(1) environmental sustainability—secures the availability and quality of natural resources. It refers to natural resource use, environmental management, pollution prevention (air, water, land, waste)
(2) social sustainability—secures the quality of life, safety, and services for citizens. It refers to the standard of living, education, community bonds, equal opportunity.
(3) economic sustainability—secures economic efficiency, profits, economic growth, research & development, technological advancements.

The three-pillar conception of (social, economic, and environmental) sustainability is commonly represented by three intersecting circles with

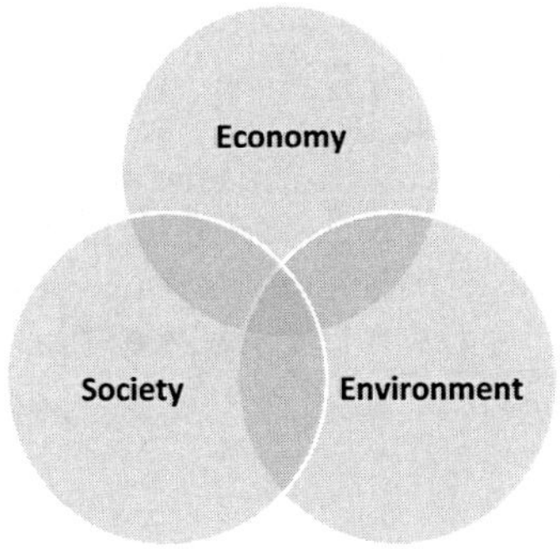

Figure 2.2 The Three Pillars of Sustainability

overall sustainability at the center. The tripartite description of sustainability is often represented in the form of three intersecting circles of society, environment, and economy, with sustainability being placed at the intersection, as shown in Figure 2.2. The three pillars themselves were explicitly embedded in their formulation (UN, 2012a).

In the model, which is adapted on a case-by-case basis, the sustainability variable α affects TC by specifically affecting one or more of the key variables of uncertainty, complexity, and/or asset specificity in a way that is shown and explained in the following chapters.

4. Conclusion

The chapter has surveyed the main concepts and methods of economic theory, and it has provided a basic, though rigorous, background to allow the reader to understand the remainder of the book. Key concepts have been defined and explained. Besides, the chapter has illustrated the key reasoning inspiring economics, based on trading-off costs and benefits of choice. The chapter has revised the concepts of scarcity, trade-offs, marginality, market equilibrium including market demand and supply formation, perfect competition market failures, externalities, public goods, monopoly, oligopoly, sustainability, among the others. In particular, the chapters have focused on the analytical framework provided by TCE, since TCE is the selected economic theory that is applied for the analysis of the case studies. According to TCE, the most efficient governance structure, associated with industrial production, including agri-food, is the one resulting from efficient transaction costs minimization. Transaction costs are the costs of running the economic system of firms (Williamson, 1979). The theory suggests that each type of transaction produces coordination costs of monitoring, controlling, and managing transactions.

They mostly depend on three key variables: (1) uncertainty of the transaction, (2) complexity of the transaction, and (3) asset specificity required by the transaction. The degree of intensity of such variables affects the level (quantitatively or qualitatively quantified) of the transaction costs, which, in turn, define the most efficient governance structure. In the end, the chapter has presented the theoretical model that is adopted for the analysis of the case studies. The model is a standard TCE model that embodies a variable representing the degree of sustainability, adopted by agri-food firms when producing high-quality outputs. Sustainability is defined based on the 2012 UN Resolution as a holistic concept, based on three pillars of society, economy, and environment. The model architecture prescribes that sustainability affects TC and contributes to determining the most TC-minimizing governance structure that coordinates production and exchange. The way this occurs is determined on a case-by-case basis in the remainder of the book.

Fixing the concepts: selected questions

- What is economics?
- What are the costs and benefits of choice?
- Why do economists think on the margin?
- Why do economists build behavioral assumptions?
- What is defined as scarcity in the economic framework?
- Why is the price mechanism an indicator of scarcity?
- Why social welfare is achieved through exchange in markets under a perfect completion structure?
- What are market failures?
- What characterizes a perfect competition?
- What are transaction costs?
- How does uncertainly relate to transaction costs?
- What are the two behavioral assumptions that the transaction economists make?
- What is opportunism? What is bounded rationality? What is asset specificity?
- When would the negotiating parties use a short-term (spot) contract?
- When would the negotiating parties use a long-term contract?
- When would the negotiating parties use vertical integration?
- Why "using the price mechanism" is costly?
- What is sustainability?

Notes

1 Externalities occur if an economic agent's activity, such as consumption or production, affects the well-being of uninvolved economic agents. The term

externality comes from the fact that someone external to the action or transaction is affected by the production of consumption of the good. There are two types of externality: a negative externality occurs if an activity creates costs (harm or discomfort) for uninvolved economic agents. A positive externality occurs if an activity creates benefits for uninvolved economic agents.

2 A monopoly is a market structure where there is a firm that is the sole seller of a product without close substitutes. Oligopoly is a market structure in which only a few sellers offer similar or identical products. The market structure is characterized by strategic behavior and interaction in oligopoly: A firm's decisions about price or quantity can affect other firms and cause them to react. The firm will consider these reactions when making decisions. The oligopolists may decide to cooperate or decide independently in a context of strategic interaction.

3 A public good is a good with two specific characteristics: (1) Non-excludability: Once the good has been produced, non-payers/free riders cannot be excluded from using and benefiting from the good. (2) Non-rivalry: The consumption of the good by one additional person does not reduce anyone else's enjoyment of the good. When a unit of a public good is produced, everyone in the market gets to consume it, irrespective of the fact whether they paid for it or not.

4 Williamson identified hybrid forms in his seminal paper in 1991. "*Whereas I was earlier of the view that transactions of the middle kind were very difficult to organize and hence were unstable, . . ., I am now persuaded that transactions in the middle range are much more common*". But it is the 1991 paper that systematized and modeled the concept of hybrids. As Menard (2004, p. 3) points out "*The vocabulary itself is not stabilized. Besides hybrids, one can read papers about clusters, networks, symbiotic arrangements, supply-chain systems, administered channels, nonstandard contracts, and so forth. My entry to this undefined set of organizations is pragmatic*". Menard (2004) attempts to define such heterogeneous typology of governance structure by highlighting empirical regularities. The author finds that "*what distinguishes (and plagues) hybrid arrangements is that these regularities are rooted in a mix of competition and cooperation that subordinates the key role played by prices in markets and by command in hierarchies. Thus. the workability of this mix depends on specific mechanisms capable of reconciling legal autonomy and interdependence. This is why these arrangements often use specialized managers for monitoring the arrangement and/or rely on arbitrators to smooth competition*" (p. 9).

5 The last two decades have witnessed a dramatic increase in the number of publications on "sustainability", to the extent where "sustainability science" is often seen as a distinct field. However, "sustainability" remains an open concept with a plethora of definitions, interpretations, and context-specific understanding. See Purvis et al. (2019) for a critical survey and references.

References

Coase, R. (1937). The Nature of the Firm. *Economica*, 16, 386–405. Blackwell Publishing.

Mankiew, G. (2001). *Principles of Economics*, Fort Worth TX Harcourt College Publisher.

Menard, C. (2004). The Economics of Hybrid Organizations. *Journal of Institutional and Theoretical Economics*, 160, 345–376.

Purvis B., Y. Mao and D. Robinson. (2019). Three Pillars of Sustainability: In Search of Conceptual Origins. *Sustainable Science*, 14, 681–695.

Robbins L. (1932). *An Essay on the Nature & Significance of Economic Science*. London McMillan.

UN (2012a). *The Future We Want*. Resolution Adopted by the General Assembly on 27 July 2012 (A/RES/66/288). United Nations, New York.

UN (2012b). Report of the United Nations Conference on Sustainable Development (A/CONF.216/16). United Nations, New York.

UN (2015). *Transforming Our World: The 2030 Agenda for Sustainable Development*. Resolution Adopted by the General Assembly on 25 September (A/RES/70/1). United Nations, New York.

Williamson, O. (1979). Transaction-Cost Economics: The Governance of Contractual Relations. *Journal of Law and Economics*, 22, 233–261.

Williamson, O. (1986). Transaction-Cost Economics: The Governance of Contractual Relations. In J. Barney and W. Ouchi (Eds.), *Organizational Economics* (pp. 98–129). San Francisco: Jossey-Bass.

Part II

Applications

Case studies that apply the analytical framework

3 The case of Parmigiano Reggiano

1. Introduction

The chapter applies the economic analysis presented in the first part of the book to the case of Parmigiano Reggiano's production and organization. The chapter is organized as follows. Section 2 describes the product and describes the main production phases. Section 3 presents key figures on Parmigiano Reggiano's market performance. Section 4 applies TCE analysis to show why the production is managed and organized in a consortium, seen as an efficient transaction costs minimizing governance structure: (2) how economic efficiency of the organization, food quality, and environmental sustainability can self-enforce and cause no trade-off in the case of Parmigiano Reggiano. Section 5 concludes the chapter.

2. The product

Article 1 of the Parmigiano Reggiano Consortium regulation (*Disciplinare*) defines Parmigiano Reggiano as:

> *a hard cheese made of rawcow's milk, which is partially skimmed by allowing the cream to rise to the surface. The cheese is scalded and slowly matured. The milk must not undergo any heat treatment and has to come from cows fed primarily on fodder obtained in the area of origin. The cheese must be matured for at least 12 months. Parmigiano Reggiano can be sold whole, in portions, or grated.*[1]

Parmigiano Reggiano is produced exclusively in the provinces of Parma, Reggio Emilia, Modena, Bologna to the left of the Reno river, and Mantua to the right of the Po river. The cheese production is based on strictly regulated standards and rules (*Disciplinare*) set by the Parmigiano Reggiano Consortium, which combines tradition and innovation, quality, excellence, and slow times, following the natural rhythm of the seasons. The production main phases are synthesized as follows.

(1) Production

To produce a typical 39.9-kilo wheel, around 520 liters of milk are used. The output from the evening and morning milking process is delivered to the dairy raw and unskimmed. The milk is poured into the traditional copper vats and mixed with the milk from the previous evening. The milk slowly and naturally coagulates with the addition of rennet and a whey starter. The curd is broken down by the master cheesemaker with the traditional tool called "*spino*" into minuscule granules. The curd then follows a cooking process, after which the cheesy granules form a single mass. After a while, the cheesemaker removes the cheese mass, which generates two twin wheels. The cheese is then cut into two parts, wrapped in the typical linen cloth, and then placed in a mold, which gives it its final shape. Each wheel is applied with a casein plate, attaching a unique and sequential alphanumeric code that allows traceability along the whole production chain. After a few hours, a special marking band engraves the month and year of production onto the cheese, the cheese factory registration number, and the dotted inscriptions around the complete circumference of the cheese wheel. After a few days, the wheels are immersed in a saturated solution of water and salt for salting by osmosis and can be sent to maturation.

(2) Maturation

The minimum maturation time is 12 months. After this period, a quality inspection is performed to check compliance with the required standards.[2] After 12 months, the experts carry out a test on all the wheels: each wheel is tapped with a hammer, and the trained ear of the quality inspector can capture any defect inside the cheese that may compromise quality. Only after this period, it can be decided if each wheel can continue the maturation up to 24, 36, 40 months, and more. The standards' conforming wheels are marked with the hot-iron brand thus becoming Parmigiano Reggiano. All identifying marks and signs are removed from any wheel that does not meet the PDO (Protected Denomination of Origin) requirements.

(3) Quality control

Quality control tackles three-cheese categories: (1) "first-grade" Parmigiano Reggiano category, under which the cheese fully complies with the production specifications; it is marked with the hot-iron brand; (2) "medium-grade" Parmigiano Reggiano category, under which the cheese shows minor or moderate defects in the structure of its paste and/or on the rind but still keeps the typical organoleptic characteristics of the product; these wheels are marked with the hot-iron brand, but they can be recognized through the parallel grooves engraved all around the cheese rind; and (3) "de-rinded" cheese category, under which the cheese shows major defects and is downgraded by eliminating the marks of origin through the removal of the rind. Therefore, this cheese cannot be called Parmigiano Reggiano. Starting from the eighteenth month of maturation, dairies may request the Consortium to add an extra mark on first-grade Parmigiano Reggiano. This is the premium or export mark that provides further indications of the quality of Parmigiano Reggiano. These marks can be affixed also on the packaging of the cheese.[3]

3. Parmigiano Reggiano-selected figures on product and market performance

Table 3.1 reports the main figures and facts related to the Parmigiano Reggiano market performance. The data are recorded in 2018, but they are (with marginal variations) representative of a sustainable trend (see Sckokai et al., 2009). The purpose of the section is simply descriptive and aims to provide a background for the analysis.

Table 3.1 is divided into three main parts. The first part provides a glance at the organization of the market. The milk producers are selected according to strict quality standards set by the Consortium. Most milk producers are organized in cooperatives that gather and sell their outputs only to the Consortium, acting as a monopsonist. At the farm level, milk price is determined by stringent production rules. Given that raw milk has virtually no alternative use in the area, and cooperatives are the dominant organizational form in the processing sector, the milk price is driven by the trend in the cooperatives' net revenues. Parmigiano cheese producers adhere to the Consortium after a scrutiny of the existence of the required participation condition. The Consortium is committed to the protection of the Designation of Origin, the facilitation of trade and consumption by promoting every initiative aimed at safeguarding the typicality, quality, and unique features of the product.

The second part of the table lists the most important production inputs and productivity. It is worth highlighting a comparison: it takes 13.5 liters of milk to produce 1 kilo of Parmigiano cheese. It takes 5 liters of milk to produce Italian fresh cow cheese (e.g., ricotta, Stracchino), and it takes, on an average, 9/10 liters to produce Italian, aged cheese (e.g., Asiago).

In the end, the last part of the table provides information on recent economic performance, prices, produced quantity, and revenues. The figures are illustrative of an extremely positive economic performance, that is

Table 3.1 Selected Figures on Market Structure and Performance

Indicator	*Numeric Figure*	*Description*
Market Structure Indicators		
Milk Suppliers	2,820	Farms have supplied milk to the dairies (2,893 in 2017, 4,500 in 2006). The number changes yearly because of the continuous quality standards monitoring, performed by the Consortium.
Cheese Producers	330	Number of farms producing Parmigiano Reggiano. They are organized in a Consortium that regulates production and quality standards
Domestic Demand	60% of production	Percentage distribution of demand. Domestic demand includes household and industrial— away from home consumption and food industry use.
International Demand	40% of production	Main importing countries: France (11,333 tons), the United States (10,493 tons), Germany (9,471 tons), the United Kingdom (6,940 tons), and Canada (3,030 tons).
Selected Production Inputs		
Milk	1.92 million tons and	The farms' total produced milk per year (represents around 16% of Italian milk production).
Cows	265,000	Number of cows (older than 24 months), producing the milk for the Parmigiano Reggiano
Labor	50,000	People involved in the Production Supply Chain
Marginal Productivity of Milk	13.5	An additional amount (1 kg) of produced cheese requires 13.5 liters of milk.
Average Productivity of Milk	2	Wheels produced by each tons of used milk in 1 year
Average Productivity of Labor	74	Wheels produced on average by a single worker in 1 year
Economic Performance Main Indicators		
Output Quantity	3,699,695	Wheels produced in 2018 (+1.35% for 2017), corresponding to 147.692 tons
Output Value	2.4	Billion Euro revenues (2018)
Price	10 (12 months) 12 (24 months) 15 (36 months)	Euro per kilo, average price

Source: Our elaboration with data from Parmigiano Reggiano Consortium[4]

stable in time. However, it is worth mentioning that the year 2018 has been considered a record year for production which increased by 1.35% over the previous year. The 3.7 million wheels of cheese (about 148 thousand tons) produced in 2018 represented the highest peak in the age-old history of Parmigiano.

4. Transaction costs economic analysis of Parmigiano Reggiano production

We recall shortly the foundations of TCE theory, presented in Chapter 1. According to TCE, the most efficient governance structure associated with industrial production including agri-food, is the one resulting from efficient transaction costs minimization. Transaction costs are the costs of running the economic system of firms (Williamson, 1979). The theory suggests that each type of transaction produces coordination costs of monitoring, controlling, and managing the transaction. They mostly depend on three key variables: (1) uncertainty of the transaction, (2) complexity of the transaction, and (3) asset specificity required by the transaction. The degree of intensity of such variables affects the level (quantitatively or qualitatively quantified) of the transaction costs, which, in turn, define the most efficient governance structure. The higher the degree of asset specificity, uncertainty, and complexity of the transactions, the lower the reliance on the (neoclassical) market mechanism (that does not guarantee the minimization of transaction costs), and the higher the reliance on hybrid and hierarchical institutional structures (see Menard, 2004).

In what follows, qualitative TCE analysis is applied by describing the content of the variables required to, in our setting, qualitatively upraise the level of transaction costs in the production of Parmigiano Reggiano cheese.

A. Behavioral assumptions

Bounded rationality

Bounded rationality implies that the economic agents cannot choose within all possible contingencies and situations because they are not familiar with all of them. In the case of Parmigiano Reggiano, producers operate with a well-known technology in a stable environment with a stable demand worldwide. Besides, some contingencies can be forecasted thanks to the millenary production of this product that has allowed the accumulation of traditional knowledge capital, based on empirical experience. The consequences of bounded rationality may be limited.

Opportunistic behavior

Opportunistic behavior is defined as a condition of seeking self-interest with guile, including hidden information and hidden actions. In this way, it is expected that some agents behave differently from what they appear to be doing. According to this definition, it is possible to state that in the case of Parmigiano Reggiano, opportunistic behavior is limited by the direct observability of the performance and input of production. For instance the quality of the final products and that of the milk provided by the milk producers can be tested with specific devices. Opportunistic behavior is also limited by the system of punishments for those who deviate from the regulation on quality standards, which incentivize credible commitment.

B. Variables affecting transaction costs

Uncertainty

Uncertainty can be defined as imperfect knowledge about an event and its outcome. The highest degree of uncertainty in this perspective refers to problems that may arise during production and is related to the possibility that the aging of the wheels does not occur properly due to natural and/or processing causes. The latter implies the impossibility to brand and commercialize the wheel as Parmigiano Reggiano. This, in turn, may affect supply price and quantity. Uncertainty may also negatively affect the fluctuations of demand that are subject to larger variances in markets where the product is not well known and competes with (potential, perceived) substitutes that are evaluated by the consumers only on the basis of price. In this perspective, for instance, Parmigiano Reggiano is much more expensive (per kilo) than other types of cheese with similar names/brands. Informed consumers are aware of the intrinsic qualitative differences between the products. Uninformed consumers are not aware of it. The informational asymmetry may increase transaction uncertainty in those markets.

The production of Parmigiano Reggiano is therefore subject to a certain extent of output and price/quantity/uncertainty. This usually applies to most transactions and might be resolved through markets. The uncertainty on the proper aging (and quality) of the wheel, on the contrary, requires a certain degree of organizational coordination.

Complexity

Complexity refers to many different dimensions related to the implementation of the transaction. Among those there is the transaction frequency, for example, the number of times the transaction is expected to take place. In the case of Parmigiano Reggiano, the frequency of transactions is high. The purchase of milk occurs daily and so does the cheese production, including daily shipping all over the world. Besides, complexity also affects the requirement to guarantee the high-quality standards of inputs and outputs to keep the high level of the cheese reputation. This requires the adoption of an effective certification mechanism; the definition and implementation of strategies aiming at monitoring, communicating, and legally protecting the reputation. The high frequency of the exchanges and the need to preserve the high reputation of the product worldwide increase complexity and require a certain degree of coordination of the transactions.

Asset specificity

There is the potential presence of different specific assets since the investments made to support a particular transaction have a higher value to that transaction than they would have if they were redeployed for any other objective. Asset specificity is a variable that refers to the characteristics of the investments that need to be done to make the product unique and which cannot be redeployed to alternative uses. The lower the asset specificity, the lower the transaction costs; while the higher the asset specificity, the higher the transaction costs. In the case of Parmigiano Reggiano, the different types of assets specificity are:

- PHYSICAL ASSETS

Physical assets are easily redeployable. Land and meadows can be used for other types of cultivations and/or cattle breeding. Industrial machinery and plants for cheese production can easily be reused for the production of different cheese and dairies. There is, therefore, a low level of physical asset specificity.

- DEDICATED ASSETS

Dedicated assets are limited.

- HUMAN ASSETS

Human assets involved are weekly specified, except for the "*mastri formaggiai*" (cheese masters). Breeders and workers, up to highly skilled managers, can be redeployed in other (agri-food) businesses and productions. *Mastri formaggiai* have accumulated knowledge capital and expertise related to the monitoring of the product during the production stages, which is not easily redeployable and is specific to anything but Parmigiano Reggiano production.

- SITE ASSETS

Site specificity plays an important role because of regulation and contractual constraints. There is a mutual, geographical dependency between milk producers and cheese producers. Parmigiano Reggiano, besides, can only be produced in a well-defined geographical area, with milk produced in a well-defined geographical area as well.

- BRAND NAME CAPITAL

The Parmigiano Reggiano brand signals a high-quality product to consumers, thus reducing their uncertainty related to information searching and quality guarantee on the product characteristics, like proper aging and nutritional content. It also conveys a clear message on the whole idiosyncratic production procedure, linked to product-specific expertise, history, and tradition. The latter is highly idiosyncratic, and therefore the brand name capital asset presents an extremely high degree of specificity.

- TEMPORAL ASSETS

Temporal specificity is high since Parmigiano Reggiano's production and quality are characterized by a precise aging process that features the existence and the essence of the product. On the other hand, production occurs daily and is highly frequent. Overall, temporal asset specificity is average.

Table 3.2 provides a qualitative assessment of the level of transaction costs that incur in the production and exchange of Parmigiano Reggiano.

C. Transaction costs minimizing governance structure: the consortium

In synthesis, brand name capital and high site asset specificity increase transaction costs. This implies and requires a certain degree of coordination in the organization of transactions, which cannot be completely performed in the markets. On the other hand, low/average levels of uncertainty and complexity and most types of asset specificities would not drive towards hierarchical structures.

In this framework, the Parmigiano Reggiano Consortium represents transaction costs minimizing governance structure. The Consortium is a "hybrid" (Williamson, 1979) structure in which the degree of specificity of several investments, uncertainty, and complexity in the transactions'

Table 3.2 Qualitative Assessment of TC for Parmigiano Reggiano

Behavioral Assumptions	
Bounded Rationality	Negligible
Opportunistic Behavior	Negligible
Variables Affecting Transaction Costs	
Uncertainty	Low/average
Complexity	Low/average
Asset Specificity	
Physical assets	Low specificity
Dedicated asset	Low specificity
Human assets	Low specificity with the exception of "*mastri formaggiai*"
Site	High specificity
Brand name capital	Very high specificity
Temporal	Average specificity

organizations are, with some exceptions, not particularly high. However, there are peculiar assets that present a high/very high degree of specificity that requires a certain degree of coordination in the organization of transactions, carried on in and by the Parmigiano Reggiano Consortium that established and monitors the respect of the rules and instructions on quality standards.

Coordination is guaranteed by the existence and action of the Consortium that sets the rules for the selection of milk and cheese producers, the rules related to the definition of the product and its production and exchange conditions, and the rules related to quality requirements. In synthesis, the regulation through the consortium becomes the key to achieve economic efficiency (TC minimizing) and to embody a certain degree of sustainability. This is illustrated in what follows. Recalling Equation (1) from Chapter 1,

$$\begin{aligned}&\textit{TC minimizing Governance Structure}\\&\quad = \min(\textit{TC}\ (\textit{uncertainty}\ (\bullet), \textit{complexity}\ (\bullet), \textit{asset specificity}\ (\bullet), \alpha))\end{aligned} \tag{1}$$

We can rewrite for the Parmigiano Reggiano case study that:

$$\begin{aligned}\textit{Consortium} = \min(&\textit{TC}\ (\textit{uncertainty}\ (K,\alpha), \textit{complexity}\ (G,\alpha),\\&\textit{asset specificity}\ (F)))\end{aligned} \tag{2}$$

Where the Consortium is the most efficient governance structure resulting from the minimization of transaction costs. In turn, transaction costs derive from uncertainty arisen from a set of variables *K* (markets with asymmetric information about the product quality; wheels aging). TC are generated by complexity that arises from a set of variables *G* (representing certification, monitoring of reputation, and compliance of quality standards). In the end, asset specificity depends on a set of variables *F* (brand name capital and high site asset specificity).

Moreover, the variable α represents sustainability. Sustainability requirements affect both the complexity and uncertainty and increase transaction costs. The organization and coordination of transactions within the Parmigiano Reggiano Consortium, however, aiming at minimizing TC through quality regulation positively affect and implement sustainability requirements, mostly in the environmental sustainability dimension. Environmental sustainability is a key factor in food quality and security. Key indicators of environmental sustainability related to Parmigiano Reggiano production cover several aspects of environmental sustainability. For instance, the milk used for producing Parmigiano Reggiano has to be procured from a local, indigenous species of the cow (like *Reggiana Rossa*). This production requirement represents a valorization and protection of cattle biodiversity. Geographical biodiversity is guaranteed by the requirement to produce Parmigiano Reggiano only in the area of origin (Parma, Reggio Emilia, Modena, Mantua, right of the Po river, Bologna, left of the Reno river) where forage is grown, and milk is produced and processed into cheese maturation and packaging.[5] In addition, the *Disciplinare* requires that the feeding of cattle complies with the norms that ban the use of silage, fermented feeds, and animal flour.[6] Additives and preservatives are banned in all phases of production.

The sustainability indicators signal an attempt to conserve local biodiversity and use sustainable production practices, even if it is more costly. For instance, the daily portion per cow costs 80 cents when fed with fresh and dry forage and 18 cents when fed with dried corn containing silage. Besides, cows are left free to graze forage in fields and meadows, contributing to the conservation of green areas. Those provisions can be interpreted as rules that not only define the quality requirements for production inputs but also environmental sustainability standards. Fodder from the defined geographical not only signals provenance and local specificity required for quality branding but also reduces negative externalities generated by public transportation. The same holds for local cows. The silage ban, also, not only aims at increasing the milk quality, but also aims at reducing the adoption of animal food that has a high environmental burden.

Economic efficiency (TC minimizing) and environmental sustainability are both guaranteed through the definition, implementation, and respect of Parmigiano Reggiano's high-quality standards.

5. Conclusion

The chapter has applied a qualitative TCE analysis to assess whether the Parmigiano Reggiano Consortium is the most efficient governance structure or not. The regulation established by the provides fundamental insights to address and (at least partially) solve uncertainty of transactions and to secure and guarantee the extremely high investment in brand capital assets, given its idiosyncratic and specificity features. A detailed description of the features of the product, in a TCE framework, allows minimizing both producers' and consumers' search and information costs.[7]

Besides, through the definition, implementation, and strict monitoring of rules, the Consortium coordinates production and commercialization and secures ex-ante-specific investment in brand capital value. Producers are informed on what the product is and what characteristics are required to brand a cheese like Parmigiano Reggiano. Consumers can correctly identify the cheese characteristics like age, milk provenience through the brand, and related certification. The investment in specific assets is (aims to be) guaranteed by the regulated organization of production, mostly aiming at the selection and use of high-quality inputs that positively affect and implement environmental sustainability. Besides, the coordination and regulation provided by and within the Consortium allow the securitization of temporal and site high specific investments by associating those investments with the idea of a high-quality product. Therefore, even if investment in quality may generate higher production costs, the regulation and coordination of production and transactions through a strict code of quality rules allow economizing on transaction costs and guaranteeing environmental sustainability.

Fixing the concepts: selected questions

- Why is the Consortium the most TC-minimizing governance structure in the case of Parmigiano Reggiano?
- Why is the Consortium implementing environmental sustainability when minimizing transaction costs?
- How do the provisions regulating the product quality affect environmental sustainability?
- Why "using the price mechanism" is costly?
- Which key variables mostly affect the degree of transaction costs in the case of Parmigiano Reggiano?

Notes

1 Article 3.2 of the *Disciplinare* strictly defines what Parmigiano Reggiano is: "'Parmigiano Reggiano' has the following characteristics:

- The cheeses are cylindrical with a slightly convex or virtually straight heel and flat faces with a slightly raised edge.
- The flat faces have a diameter of 35–45 cm and the heel height is 20–26 cm.
- The minimum weight of each cheese is 30 kg.
- The outer rind is a natural straw color.
- The rind is approximately 6-mm thick.
- The body of the cheese is between light straw-colored and straw-colored.
- The cheese's characteristic aroma and taste are fragrant, delicate, and flavorsome without being pungent.
- The body of the cheese is fine-grained and flaky in texture.
- The minimum fat content in dry matter is 32%.
- The cheese contains no additives.
- It has a cyclopropane fatty acid ratio of less than 22 mg per 100 g of fat (already accounting for the uncertainty of measurement, gas chromatography-mass spectrometry (CG-MS) method).
- The minimum 12-month maturing period must take place in the defined geographical area".

2 During maturation, thanks to the action of the enzymes released by lactic bacteria, proteins are broken down into smaller pieces, free peptides, and amino acids.
3 Source: Our Elaboration with Parmigiano Reggiano Consortium Data (www.parmigiano-reggiano.it/).
4 www.parmigianoreggiano.com.
5 Article 3.4 establishes that: "*The farms that rear the dairy cows whose milk is to be processed into 'Parmigiano Reggiano' must be located within the defined geographical area. The milk must be produced and processed within the defined geographical area*".
6 In particular, Article 3.3 of the *Disciplinare* states the conditions for quality feed and raw materials: "*The cows are to be fed primarily on fodder from the defined geographical area, specified by quantity and quality. At least 75 % of fodder dry matter must be produced within the geographical area. Feedstuffs may make up at most 50 % of the dry matter of the feed ration. The use of silage of any kind is banned. Cow's milk, salt, calf rennet. The milk is from cows reared in the defined geographical area*".
7 For instance, Article 3.5 sets the commercialization and use rules:

> "*Parmigiano Reggiano' can be sold whole, in portions or grated. In the interests of consumer protection, to guarantee the authenticity of pre-packaged, grated, or portioned 'Parmigiano Reggiano' placed on the market, grating, portioning and subsequent packaging must take place in the defined geographical area. This is necessary because the markings that identify a whole cheese as 'Parmigiano Reggiano' are lost or are not visible on grated cheese or portions, so the origin of the pre-packaged product has to be guaranteed. This is also necessary because the cheese needs to be packaged quickly after portioning and using procedures that prevent it from becoming dehydrated or oxidized, or from losing its original 'Parmigiano Reggiano' organoleptic characteristics. Cutting into a wheel of cheese deprives the cheese of the natural protection afforded by the rind, which – itself being highly dehydrated – insulates the cheese very well against the surrounding environment. Only the whole cheese bearing the protected designation of origin 'Parmigiano*

> *Reggiano' may be grated. It must be packaged immediately after grating and may not be subject to any processing or have any substance added to it that could affect how long the cheese keeps for or its original organoleptic characteristics. 'Parmigiano Reggiano' portions may be packaged at the same business premises on which they are cut*".

Article 3.6 states the conditions for branding.

> "*The identity markings found on each 'Parmigiano Reggiano' cheese are the words 'Parmigiano-Reggiano' in pin-dot writing, together with the registration number of the dairy that produced it and the year and month of production, which are applied to the surface of the heel using stencils (marking strips). The cheeses also bear an oval stamp with the words 'Parmigiano Reggiano Consorzio Tutela', a casein nameplate with the codes identifying the cheese, and, as the case may be, the markings identifying a second-class cheese. Pre-packaged, grated, and portioned 'Parmigiano Reggiano' cheese placed on the market is identified by a logo depicting a segment and wheel of 'Parmigiano Reggiano' cheese next to a knife, with the words 'PARMIGIANO REGGIANO' appearing below. This marking, which is a mandatory component of the label, must be displayed in accordance with the technical specifications defined by the Consortium in the relevant agreement*".

References

Menard, C. (2004). The Economics of Hybrid Organizations. *Journal of Institutional and Theoretical Economics*, 160, 345–376.

Sckokai, P., C. Soregaroli and M. Daniele (2009). Estimating Market Power by Retailers in the Italian Parmigiano Reggiano and Grana Padano Cheese Market, No 51425, Conference, August 16–22, International Association of Agricultural Economists, Beijing, China.

Williamson, O. (1979). Transaction-Cost Economics: The Governance of Contractual Relations. *Journal of Law and Economics*, 22, 233–261.

4 The case of Mozzarella di Bufala Campana

1. Introduction

This chapter applies the economic analysis presented in the first part of the book to the case of Mozzarella di Bufala Campana production and organization. The chapter is organized as follows. Section 2 describes the product and describes the main production phases. Section 3 presents key figures on the Mozzarella di Bufala Campana market performance and production. Section 4 applies TCE analysis to show (1) why the production is managed and organized in a consortium, seen as an efficient transaction costs minimizing governance structure; (2) how economic efficiency of the organization, food quality, and environmental sustainability can self-enforce and cause no trade-off in the case of Mozzarella di Bufala Campana. Section 5 concludes the chapter.

2. The product

Mozzarella di Bufala Campana (PDO) is a fresh cheese, produced with the exclusive use of fresh whole buffalo milk from breeding farms located in the certified area (Naples, Caserta, and Salerno in the Campania region in the South-west of Italy; Foggia in Apulia and an area in the South of the Lazio region). Article 3 of the *Disciplinare* defines what Mozzarella[1] di Bufala is and lists all the characteristics the cheese must own to be labeled as Mozzarella di Bufala Campana. The geographical provenience of the milk and the geographical location of the cheese farm in a territory defined by the *Disciplinare* are necessary but not sufficient conditions to identify the product.[2]

Production is organized as follows. After the milk produced by the farms is transported to the production firms and undergoes all the sanitary controls and checks, a traditional processing scheme of buffalo mozzarella follows, which can be divided into two phases. In the first phase, the preparation of the curd and the subsequent maturation under whey are carried out until it reaches a sufficient acidity to be subjected to stretching. In the second, the acidified curd is spun to take on the characteristic filamentary structure of buffalo mozzarella with spun paste. The milk is poured into a cauldron and warmed up to around 35 degrees Celsius. At this point, the natural calf rennet is added to the milk, which has to "rest" for an hour. After a few minutes, when the milk has coagulated due to the rennet, the cheesy lumps are broken with a tool called "*spino*", which reduces them to just over the size of a walnut. From this moment. the separation between the solid and the liquid phase of the milk occurs. The liquid product, removed by withdrawal, is called "sweet whey", while the solid product is called curd. The latter is left to acidify under the whey until it is defined as "mature" or "ready" for spinning by the cheesemaker, using the spinning test that he performs. Testing of the filature implies adding boiling water to about half a kilo of shredded curd, which is blended until it melts and is then stretched by hand using a wooden stick: if it evenly stretches without breaking it is judged "ready" for the next spinning phase. The curd that reached the right degree of maturation is placed on tables where the whole residual whey is purged. It is then cut into strips and placed in special containers still today made of wood and called "*mastelli*", where boiling water is added. The contact between boiling water and curd causes the fusion of the mass, which is continuously raised and pulled until a single homogeneous body is obtained. When the spinning is at the right point, once the water is removed, the *pasta filata* is taken and "cut" into the desired size. Once the portions are made, they are passed in cold water and then left in brine. For making the portions, an important part of the shaping phase is carried out manually by the cheesemaker and his collaborators. The remaining part involves the use of molding machines that produce pieces with a predetermined weight. The Mozzarella di Bufala Campana produced in this way is first left in tanks containing cold water to ensure a first important firming process. It is then moved into other tanks also containing salt solutions and that complete the process by giving the right degree of flavor to the product. Forming, salting, and packaging of buffalo mozzarella complete the processing cycle.

3. Mozzarella di Bufala Campana-selected figures on product and market performance

Table 4.1 reports the main figures and facts related to Mozzarella di Bufala Campana, according to the available data. The purpose of this section is simply descriptive and informative, and it aims to provide a background for the analysis.

Table 4.1 is divided into three main parts. The first part provides selected information on the market structure (number of breeders, number of producers) and performance (import/export). The second part of the table lists

Table 4.1 Selected Figures on Market Structure and Performance

Indicator	*Numeric Figure*	*Description*
Market Structure Indicators		
Producers	1,274	Number of Mozzarella di Bufala Campana production firms
Breeders	1,267	Number of buffalo breeders
Domestic Demand	65.86% of production	Percentage distribution of demand. Domestic demand includes household and industrial—away from home consumption and food industry use
International Demand	34.14% of production	Main importing countries: The Netherlands, France, Germany, Spain, the United Kingdom, and the United States
Selected Production Inputs		
Buffalo Heads	400,792	Number of buffalo heads in Italy (2018). Around three quarters of buffalo heads are raised in Campania, about 18% in Lazio, and a further 2.6% in Puglia. Campania and Lazio, therefore, together cover about 93% of the buffaloes present in Italy.
	270,000	Number of buffalo heads that produce Mozzarella di Bufala Campana. Considering only the animals with the DOP certification, over 210 thousand (78.4%) are bred in Campania, mostly concentrated in the provinces of Caserta with almost 139 thousand animals and Salerno with over 67 thousand. In Lazio, about 52 thousand heads are bred (19%), almost all located in the provinces of Latina (over 34 thousand heads) and Frosinone (about 17 thousand). Overall, therefore, the four provinces of Caserta, Salerno, Latina, and Frosinone represent more than 95% of the buffaloes that are part of the buffalo mozzarella from Campania DOP.
Buffalo Milk	2 million quintals	2018 production: The percentage share of Campania is just under 85%, while that of Lazio stands at 12.2%. In relation to the total production of cow and buffalo milk, the percentage share of buffalo is approximately 48% in Campania and 6.4% in Lazio.

Indicator	*Numeric Figure*	*Description*
Labor	11,200	Number of workers employed in the sector (1.5% of the total employment in the provinces of Caserta and Salerno)
Milk Productivity	0.25	Milk marginal productivity: 1 additional liter of milk produces around 0.25 kilos of mozzarella.
Buffalo Productivity	186	Buffalo average productivity: 186 tons of milk per cow
Labor Productivity	4,443	Average productivity: 4,443 tons per worker
Economic Performance Main Indicators		
Output Quantity	50,212 million	Tons of produced output in 2019
Output Value	577	Million Euro Revenues (2019)
Price	13–16	Wholesale prices per kilo in Euro

Source: Our elaboration with data from Mozzarella di Bufala Campana Consortium[3]

the most important production inputs and inputs productivity. The last part of the table provides information on recent economic performance, prices, produced quantity, and revenues. The figures are illustrative of an extremely positive economic performance that is increasing in time. In 25 years, the production has more than quadrupled with an average annual growth of 6%. The economic benefits reflected in the surrounding area are not limited only to companies active in the production of mozzarella, but also concern, with different intensity, the entire supply chain, for the most part located in the proximity of the firms adhering to the Consortium. It is interesting to highlight that for every Euro of product invoiced by the members of the Consortium, 2.1 Euro are created in the local economic system.

4. Transaction costs economics analysis of Mozzarella di Bufala Campana

We recall shortly the foundations of TCE theory, presented in Chapter 1. According to TCE, the most efficient governance structure, associated with industrial production, including agri-food, is the one resulting from efficient transaction costs minimization. Transaction costs are the costs of running the economic system of firms (Williamson, 1979). The theory suggests that each type of transaction produces coordination costs of monitoring, controlling, and managing transactions. They mostly depend on three key variables: (1) uncertainty of the transaction, (2) complexity of the transaction, and (3) asset specificity required by the transaction. The degree of intensity of such variables affects the level (quantitatively or qualitatively quantified) of the transaction costs, which, in turn, define the most efficient governance structure. The higher the degree of asset specificity, uncertainty, and complexity of the transactions, the lower the reliance on the (neoclassical) market mechanism (that does not guarantee the minimization of transaction costs), and the higher the reliance on hybrid and hierarchical institutional structures (see Menard. 2004).

In what follows, qualitative TCE analysis is applied by describing the content of the variables required to, in our setting, qualitatively upraise the level of transaction costs in the production of Mozzarella di Bufala Campana.

A. Behavioral assumptions

Bounded rationality

Bounded rationality implies that the economic agents cannot choose within all possible contingencies and situations since they are not familiar with all of them. In the case of the production of Mozzarella di Bufala Campana, cheese producers operate with a well-known technology in a stable environment with a stable demand worldwide. The consequences of bounded rationality may be limited.

Opportunistic behavior

Opportunistic behavior is defined as a condition of seeking self-interest with guile, including hidden information and hidden actions. In this way, it is expected that some agents behave differently from what they appear to be doing.

According to this definition, it is possible to state that in the case of Mozzarella di Bufala Campana, opportunistic behavior is partially limited by the direct observability of the performance and input of production and by the system of punishments for those who deviate from the regulation on quality standards, which incentivize credible commitment, and by the control mechanisms implemented by the Consortium.

However, the territory of the production of Mozzarella di Bufala Campana is characterized by the existence and persistence of associations for illegal purposes that may incentivize and spur opportunistic behavior through illegal means like threats, blackmail, and ransom (Visco, 2015). This kind of opportunistic behavior might negatively affect both the volume/value of production and the reputational capital associated with the product and the geographical area of production. In this perspective, the members of the Consortium for the Protection of the Mozzarella di Bufala Campana PDO unanimously approved the Code of Ethics on July 27, 2012, during the annual assembly. The assembly was held for the first time in a property confiscated from the Camorra clan in Castel Volturno, which became the headquarters of the national training center of the State Forestry Corps. After the introduction of the Code of Ethics to be a member of the Protection Consortium, one is required to submit official anti-mafia certification before the end of each calendar year. Furthermore, severe restrictions apply for those who wish to be a part of the Consortium—they must commit to maintaining fair and loyal behavior.

B. *Variables affecting transaction costs*

Uncertainty

Uncertainty can be defined as imperfect knowledge about an event and its outcome. In the case of Mozzarella di Bufala Campana, uncertainty is moderate, even if not negligible. The production process is not characterized by the occurrence of unexpected events, like for instance hail in the case of wine-grapes harvesting. This also applies to the variables impacting demand, since the product demand is increasing worldwide. Uncertainty is also low relative to the ability to identify the product offered with certainty, which is recognizable and well regulated.

Complexity

Complexity refers to many different dimensions related to the implementation of the transaction. Concerning frequency, it is extremely high and characterized by a short production cycle. This decreases the transaction complexity. Regulatory steps increase complexity with the purpose to identify the product and protect the quality. The *Disciplinare* sets stringent rules aiming at regulating production stages. However, those rules simply codify the traditional knowledge and do not add obligations that are external to the output production stages and the used technology. Amarone della Valpolicella *Disciplinare*, for instance, regulates the frequency and type of treatment against biotic threats, adding (regulatory-based) complexity to the transaction.

The regulation of the product name brand to be associated with the Mozzarella di Bufala Campana producer label is, on the contrary, strictly regulated. This adds complexity to the transaction with the view to protect the product identity and idiosyncrasy. In this perspective, a representative of the Consortium, after having checked all regularities, applies the brand "Mozzarella di Bufala Campana" on the packaging before the product is marketed. The PDO brand is well identified and described by the *Disciplinare*. It has to represent a red sun, a blackhead of a buffalo. The indication "Mozzarella di Bufala" is written in white color and the adjective Campana in green color. The introduction of the code of ethics, aiming at minimizing potential negative impacts generated by opportunistic behavior, also increases complexity. The *Disciplinare* includes a stringent environmental regulation with the ban on the use of additives, preservatives, inhibitors, and dyes.

Asset specificity

There is the potential presence of different specific assets since the investments made to support a particular transaction have a higher value to that transaction than they would have if they were redeployed for any other objective. Asset specificity is a variable that refers to the characteristics of the investments that need to be done to make the product unique and which cannot be redeployed to alternative uses. The lower the asset specificity, the lower the transaction costs; while the higher the asset specificity, the higher the transaction costs. In the case of Mozzarella di Bufala Campana, the different types of assets specificity are given here.

• PHYSICAL ASSETS

Physical assets are easily redeployable. Land and meadows can be used for other types of animal breeding. Industrial machinery and plants easily are reused for the production of different dairies. There is, therefore, a low level of physical asset specificity.

• DEDICATED ASSETS

Dedicated assets are negligible.

• HUMAN ASSETS

Human assets involved are weakly specific, with the exception of specialized "*mastri formaggiai*".

• SITE ASSETS

Site specificity plays an important role because of regulation and contractual constraints (i.e., Article 1 of the *Disciplinare*). The site specificity extends to the milk and the cheese production.

• BRAND NAME CAPITAL

The brand signals a high-quality product to consumers. In the case at issue, the brand name refers to the product that can be branded with different labels, associated with the producer/dairy farm. For this reason, the brand-name capital asset presents an average high degree of specificity. On the contrary, a "product" asset specificity is extremely high. In particular, the product name capital is protected with a particular label that adds to the producers' brand name. This implies that the investment in brand capital is not easily redeployed.

• TEMPORAL ASSETS

Temporal specificity is low and limited by the high frequency of production. The cheese does not require aging.

Table 4.2 provides an assessment of the level of transaction costs that incur in the production and exchange of Mozzarella di Bufala Campana. The indicators synthesize the information qualitatively.

Table 4.2 Qualitative Assessment of TC for Mozzarella di Bufala Campana

Behavioral Assumptions	
Bounded Rationality	Negligible
Opportunistic Behavior	Potentially high
Variables Affecting Transaction Costs	
Uncertainty	Low
Complexity	Average
Asset Specificity	
Physical assets	Low specificity
Dedicated asset	Low specificity
Human assets	Low specificity
Site	High specificity
Brand name capital	High specificity
Temporal	Low specificity

C. *Transaction costs minimizing governance structure: the Consortium*

In opportunistic behavior, average complexity, brand name, and high site asset specificity increase transaction costs. This implies and requires a certain degree of coordination in the organization of transactions, which cannot be completely performed in the markets. On the other hand, low/average levels of uncertainty and most types of asset specificities would not drive towards hierarchical structures.

In this framework, the Consortium of Mozzarella di Bufala Campana represents a transaction-cost-minimizing governance structure. The Consortium is a "hybrid" (Williamson, 1979) structure in which the degree of specificity of several investments and the uncertainty in the organization of the transactions are, with some exceptions, not particularly high. However, there are peculiar assets that present a high/very high degree of specificity. Moreover, the strict regulatory requirements that organize production and characterize input dramatically increase complexity. This generates the need for a certain degree of coordination in the organization of transactions, carried on in and by the Consortium that establishes and monitors the respect of the rules and instructions on quality standards through the Consortium protocol (*Disciplinare*). Coordination, in turn, is guaranteed by the existence and action of the Consortium that sets the rules for the selection of milk providers and cheese producers, the rules related to the definition of the product and its production and exchange conditions, and the rules related to quality requirements. In synthesis, the regulation through the consortium becomes the key to achieve economic efficiency (TC minimizing). This is illustrated in what follows. Recalling Equation (1) from Chapter 1,

$$\textit{TC minimizing Governance Structure} = \min(\textit{TC}\ (\textit{uncertainty}\ (\bullet), \textit{complexity}\ (\bullet), \textit{asset specificity}\ (\bullet), \alpha)) \quad (1)$$

We can rewrite for the Mozzarella di Bufala Campana case study that:

$$\textit{Consortium} = \min(\textit{TC}\ (\textit{complexity}\ (G,\alpha), \textit{asset specificity}\ (F))) \quad (2)$$

where the Consortium is the most efficient governance structure resulting from the minimization of transaction costs. In turn, transaction costs derive from the complexity that arises from a set of variables G (which represent a strict regulation on all stages of production, the brand label, and regulation of the code of ethics introduced to contrast potentially high opportunistic behavior). In the end, asset specificity depends on a set of variables F (product name capital and high site asset specificity).

The variable α represents sustainability. In the case of Mozzarella di Bufala Campana, sustainability requirements affect the complexity and contribute to increasing transaction costs. The organization and coordination of transactions within Mozzarella di Bufala Campana Consortium positively affect and implement sustainability requirements, mostly in the social dimension. The potential negative impacts, generated by opportunistic behavior, are minimized by the code of ethical conduct that sets stringent ethical prerequisites for adhering to the Consortium and therefore for being able to produce Mozzarella di Bufala Campana. This is a radical position for the protection of the product quality and high excellence that are certified at the level of the ethical and moral depth of the producer, acting in a geographical area plagued by the existence of crime associations. The requirement to organize and coordinate the production and the transactions in a Consortium achieves both economic efficiency through transaction costs minimization and social sustainability.

5. Conclusion

The chapter has applied a qualitative TCE analysis to assess whether the Mozzarella di Bufala Campana Consortium is the most efficient governance structure that coordinates production stages to achieve high quality. The main findings show that the degree of complexity/frequency, brand name, and site asset specificity that affects the level of TC is mostly linked to the "unicity" of the product and the requirement to keep the quality standards. Through the definition, implementation, and strict monitoring of rules, the Consortium coordinates production and commercialization and secures ex-ante specific investment in site and brand capital value, which in this case is declined in the case of "product capital value", since the Mozzarella di Bufala Campana can be branded with different labels carrying the name of the producers. The high degree of complexity is generated by stringent rules set in the *Disciplinare*. Those rules dramatically increase ex-ante TC but are fundamental to clearly define the product identity, quality, and excellence. Most importantly, however, complexity is increased by the adoption of a code of ethical conduct that aims at minimizing the impacts of opportunistic behavior. This affects the existence and dimension of TC and the complexity of the organization. In this perspective, the Consortium represents the most efficient, hybrid structure for coordinating and regulating transaction costs (in the case at issue mostly generated by complexity). By regulating the quality, the Consortium also preserves sustainability with an emphasis on social sustainability.

Fixing the concepts: selected questions

- Why is the Consortium the most TC-minimizing governance structure in the case of Mozzarella di Bufala Campana?
- Why is the Consortium implementing social sustainability when minimizing transaction costs?
- How do the provisions regulating product quality affect social sustainability?
- Why "using the price mechanism" is costly?
- What is the role of opportunistic behavior in determining the incidence of transaction costs in the case of Mozzarella di Bufala Campana?

Notes

1 Mozzarella derives from the Italian verb *mozzare*, an operation consisting of forging the piece of filata curd by hand, detaching the single mozzarella balls with the forefinger and thumb. This is how the typical round shape of the mozzarella is obtained.

2 The *Disciplinare* sets very stringent norms aiming at defining all aspects of production in a very careful and precise way. It covers (1) the regulation of the milk, (2) the regulation of the "geographical provenience" of milk and cheese, (3) the regulation of the production phases, and (4) the definition of the product.

(1) Regulation of the milk is done by conforming to the following conditions:

- whole, raw, and fresh buffalo milk is required;
- it has to come from buffalos that are enrolled in a special registry; bred in the specified geographical areas and according to specified breeding (grazing in fenced outdoor paddocks). The buffalo is subjected to a "confined type of breeding", which limits the space available to buffaloes in order to coordinate the production phases.
- milk must have a minimum fat content of 7.2% and a minimum protein content of 4.2%.

- the milk must be filtered with traditional methods and delivered to the dairy within 60 hours from the milking.

(2) Regulation of the "geographical provenience" of milk and cheese is done by conforming to the following condition:

- The milk must come from and the cheese has to be made in defined geographical areas, as listed in Article 1.

(3) Regulation of the production phases is done by conforming to the following conditions:

- acidification of milk and curd is obtained by the addition of natural grafting serum resulting from previous processing of buffalo milk in the same dairy or in those in neighboring areas.
- temperature of boiling the milk for coagulation spans from 33°C to 37°C.
- coagulation only with natural calf rennet: curd "maturation" must take around 5 hours.
- All stages of traditional production phases are described in the *Disciplinare*. The used water has to be drinkable; the brand has to be put in the dairy; and the cheese has to be conserved in acidic liquid.

(4) Regulation of the product is done by conforming to the following conditions:

- Shape: round, "treccia" (braid), "bocconcini", "perline" "ciliegine", "nodini" "ovoline".
- Weight: from 10 to 800 grams; 3 kilos for "braids".
- Look: white porcelain color, 1 millimeter of crust, smooth surface never slimy nor hurled.
- Fat content: minimum 52%.
- Humidity: up to 65%.
- Cheese paste: thin leaf structure, slightly elastic in the first 8–10 hours of production, with no defects. When cut, it produces a slight whitish serum that has the scent of lactic ferments.

3 https://www.mozzarelladop.it.

References

Menard, C. (2004). The Economics of Hybrid Organizations. *Journal of Institutional and Theoretical Economics*, 160, 345–376.

Visco (2015). Prevenzione e contrasto della criminalità organizzata Audizione del Governatore della Banca d'Italia, Banca d'Italia.

Williamson, O. (1979). Transaction-Cost Economics: The Governance of Contractual Relations. *Journal of Law and Economics*, 22, 233–261.

5 The case of Conegliano Valdobbiadene Prosecco Superiore DOCG

1. Introduction

The chapter applies the economic analysis presented in the first part of the book to the case of Conegliano Valdobbiadene Prosecco Superiore DOCG (Prosecco for the sake of simplicity) production and organization. The chapter is organized as follows. Section 2 describes the product and the main production phases. Section 3 presents key figures on the Prosecco market performance and production. Section 4 applies TCE analysis to show why the production is managed and organized in a consortium, seen as an efficient transaction costs minimizing governance structure: (2) how economic efficiency of the organization, food quality, and environmental sustainability can self-enforce and no cause trade-off in the case of Prosecco. Section 5 concludes the chapter.

2. The product

Prosecco is an Italian sparkling or semi-sparkling white wine, mainly made from "*Glera*" grapes (Article 1 of the Consortium *Disciplinare*). Although the name is derived from that of the Italian village of Prosecco near Trieste, where the grapes may have originated, Prosecco is mostly produced in the region of Veneto, mainly in Treviso province in the North East of Italy. *Glera* has been cultivated around Conegliano and Valdobbiadene hills, now a UNESCO site, since the 18th century, but Prosecco's success begins only in the last decades after its massive production as sparkling and semi-sparkling wine. There are three different types of Prosecco: Prosecco DOC, or plain Prosecco; Prosecco DOCG; or hills Prosecco and Cartizze. In this chapter, we focus on Conegliano Valdobbiadene Prosecco Superiore DOCG. The distinction was legally stated in 2009. With the reorganization of the Prosecco denominations, the Ministry of Agriculture classified Conegliano Valdobbiadene as a *Denominazione di Origine Controllata e Garantita* (D.O.C.G.) area, the highest level of quality for Italian wines.

The production is organized in the way regulated by Article 7 of the *Disciplinare* and is summarized in what follows.

After the harvest, the *Glera* grapes are selected and transferred to the cellar for vinification and collected in steel tanks. The grapes, thanks to the gravity fall system (*sistema di caduta per gravità*), arrive at pressing step intact with all their aromatic load. Subsequently, with the aid of pneumatic presses that act in an ultra-soft way, the grapes are pressed to extract the must that is brought to the tanks for decantation. The temperature is established at around 14°C to maintain the organoleptic characteristics typical of *Glera*. At the end of the operation, the clear part of the must, with the addition of selected native yeasts, begins the alcoholic fermentation. This stage of production takes place for about 10 to 12 days in steel tanks at a constant temperature of 15–18°C. At the end of this process, the resulting output is ready to be made sparkling. The sparkling wine is made with the Charmat/*Martinotti* method (the *autoclave* method) that implies a second round of fermentation. The second fermentation takes place thanks to the use of *autoclaves*, where the base wine is mixed with cane sugar and selected native yeasts. Autoclaves are a pressurized tank that must reach a pressure of 6 atmospheres to obtain the sparkling wine, and the temperature of the wine is reduced to zero degrees; in this way, the fermentation stops, the yeast no longer eats the sugars, and releases the softness. The bubble is refined. The procedure involves refermentation for at least 40/50 days, while taking care of the fact that the process is slow and gradual to enhance the *perlage* and not stress the wine. In this part of the productive process, the input and expertise of the oenologists are crucial for the success of the final product. The alcohol content reaches 11%–11.5% volumes of alcohol starting from a base wine of about 10%–10.5% vol. At the end of the sparkling process, the product is bottled, and according to the concentration of sugars per gram/liter, it is classified according to the different types of brut, dry, and extra dry. The final product characteristics are described in Article 6.[1] After 30 days of bottle aging, the wine is ready to be marketed.

3. Prosecco DOCG-selected figures on product and market performance

Table 5.1 reports the main figures and facts related to Prosecco DOCG, according to the available data. The purpose of the section is simply descriptive and informative, and it aims to provide a background for the analysis.

Table 5.1 is divided into three main parts. The first part provides selected information on the market structure (number of winegrowers and winemakers) and performance (import/export). The second part of the table lists the

Table 5.1 Selected Figures on Market Structure and Performance

Indicator	*Numeric Figure*	*Description*
Market Structure Indicators		
Producers	438	Number of vinifying companies
	178	Number of sparkling wine producers
	3,364	Number of winegrowers
	16	Number of winegrowers' cooperatives
Domestic Demand	59.14% of production	Percentage distribution of demand. Domestic demand includes household and industrial—away from home consumption and food industry use
International Demand	40.86% of production	Main importing countries: the United States, Germany, UK
Selected Production Inputs		
Land	7,549	Hectares of land cultivated with Glera grapes
Land Productivity	11,973	Average land productivity (measured as number of bottles per ha)
Labor	6,325	Number of workers employed in the sector.
Labor Productivity	14,290	Average labor productivity measured as number of bottles per unit of labor force)
Economic Performance Main Indicators		
Output Quantity	90,382,800	Number of bottles produced in 2019
Output Value	524	Million Euro Revenues (2019)
Price	3.5–6	Wholesale prices per liter in Euro

Source: Our elaboration with data from Conegliano Valdobbiadene Prosecco DOCG Consortium[2]

most important production inputs. The last part of the table provides information on recent economic performance, prices, produced quantities, and revenues.

4. Transaction costs economic analysis of Conegliano Valdobbiadene Prosecco DOCG

We recall shortly the foundations of TCE theory, as presented in Chapter 1. According to TCE, the most efficient governance structure, associated with industrial production including agri-food, is the one resulting from efficient transaction costs minimization. Transaction costs are the costs of running the economic system of firms (Williamson, 1979). The theory suggests that each type of transaction produces coordination costs of monitoring, controlling, and managing transactions. They mostly depend on three key variables: (1) uncertainty of the transaction, (2) complexity of the transaction, and (3) asset specificity required by the transaction. The degree of intensity of such variables affects the level (quantitatively or qualitatively quantified) of the transaction costs, which, in turn, define the most efficient governance structure. The higher the degree of asset specificity, uncertainty, and complexity of the transactions, the lower the reliance on the (neoclassical) market mechanism (that does not guarantee the minimization of transaction costs), and the higher the reliance on hybrid and hierarchical institutional structures (see Menard, 2004).

In what follows, qualitative TCE analysis is applied by describing the content of the variables required to, in our setting, qualitatively upraise the level of transaction costs in the production of Conegliano Valdobbiadene Prosecco DOCG.

A. Behavioral assumptions

Bounded rationality

Bounded rationality implies that the economic agents cannot choose within all possible contingencies and situations since they are not familiar with all of them. In the case of the production of Conegliano Valdobbiadene Prosecco DOCG, wine producers operate with a well-known technology in a stable environment with an increasing demand worldwide. The consequences of bounded rationality may be limited.

Opportunistic behavior

Opportunistic behavior is defined as a condition of seeking self-interest with guile, including hidden information and hidden actions. In this way, it is expected that some agents behave differently from what they appear to be doing. In the case of Prosecco, opportunistic behavior is also limited by the direct observability of the performance and input of production and by the system of punishments for those who deviate from the regulation on quality standards, applied both for the final output and the grapes' selection, which incentivize credible commitment. However, in the case of Prosecco, the incentive to deviate from the strict regulation might be higher, since production occurs once per year. Also, the Prosecco outcome mostly depends on the quality of the grapes and the expertise of the oenologists that "make" the wine by carefully calibrating the proportion of yeast and sugars. In some cases, the oenologist might (hypothetically) act opportunistically and use yeast and sugar proportions in ways that accelerate fermentation to quicken production and marketing at the costs of altering the features that identify the Prosecco DOCG and, therefore, violating the *Disciplinare* regulation.

B. Variables affecting transaction costs

Uncertainty

Uncertainty can be defined as imperfect knowledge about an event and its outcome. In the case of Prosecco DOCG, uncertainty is moderate, even if not negligible. Uncertainty on the production process is mostly impacted by climatic conditions, abiotic and biotic threats, whose impacts cannot be predicted with certainty. Prosecco is produced once per year, and unexpected circumstances might occur that negatively impact the fermentation or the sparkling process therefore negatively impacting the outcome in terms of quality and volume of production.

Complexity

Complexity refers to many different dimensions related to the implementation of the transaction. Complexity is low relative to the ability to identify with certainty the product offered, when the product is recognizable and well regulated. Regulatory provisions increase the complexity with the twofold purpose to (1) protect and guarantee the product's high quality and (2) avoid product mystifications. Concerning point (1), the *Glera* winegrowers' regulation for the conferment of the grapes to the Prosecco wineries sets disincentives and punishments for those who do not deliver high-quality grapes or do not respect schedules and procedures. The regulation aiming at combating potential mystifications is also very stringent. There is a supervisory committee that has the task of checking that all the steps are carried out in accordance with the regulations. Once the base wine is ready, the winery must define the types of Prosecco it intends to make (brut, dry, extra dry) and list the sugar and yeast it intends to use. For both sugar and yeast, the type and quantity must also be indicated.

With 1 week's notice, the winery must notify the commission and indicate the exact day and time in when it intends to proceed with the passage of the wine in the autoclave. On the agreed day, at the agreed time, a member of the supervisory committee must be present in the cellar to check that all the steps are followed as previously declared by the cellar itself; once everything has been checked, the representative of the commission gives the approval to proceed with the sparkling process. The winery cannot proceed with the passage in an autoclave without the presence of a "controller". Each time an autoclave declares that a white wine is bottled to become Prosecco (whether DOC or DOCG), the winery must notify the fraud repression commission; a member of the commission goes to the cellar and takes seven samples from the autoclave and proceeds with the chemical, tasting, visual, and olfactory analysis to confirm that the wine in question is in line with the standards defined for Prosecco. At this point, the cellar can proceed with bottling. There is a great deal of attention given to the quality of the grapes conferred even within cooperatives.

The regulation of relations between members, the mutual purpose, and in general all that nexus regulating the relations of human capital and quality present the most important levels of complexity that might increase transaction costs. These transaction costs, generated by strict regulation, increase the complexity for the sake of high quality and high reputation standards' preservation.

Asset specificity

There is the potential presence of different specific assets since the investments made to support a particular transaction have a higher value to that transaction than they would have if they were redeployed for any other objective. Asset specificity is a variable that refers to the characteristics of the investments that need to be done to make the product unique and which cannot be redeployed to alternative uses. The lower the asset specificity, the lower the transaction costs; while the higher the asset specificity, the higher the transaction costs. In the case of Prosecco DOCG, the different types of assets specificity are:

- PHYSICAL ASSETS

Physical assets are easily redeployable. Land and meadows can be used for other types of grapes' cultivation. Industrial machinery and plants easily are reused for the production of different wines. There is, therefore, a low level of physical asset specificity.

- DEDICATED ASSETS

Dedicated assets are associated with the investments for purchasing the "*autoclave*".

- HUMAN ASSETS

Human assets involved are weakly specific, with an exception of specialized "oenologists" who are fundamental to Prosecco production.

- SITE ASSETS

Site specificity plays an important role because of regulation and contractual constraints (i.e., Article 2 of the *Disciplinare*). The site specificity extends to both the Glera grapes' cultivation and Prosecco DOCG production. In particular, according to Article 5, paragraph 2 of the *Disciplinare*, the operations of preparation of sparkling wine, that is the oenological practices for the second fermentation and the stabilization, the sweetening in the types, when allowed, as well as the bottling and packaging operations must be carried out in the territory of the province of Treviso.

- BRAND NAME CAPITAL

The brand signals a high-quality product to consumers. In the case at issue, the brand name refers to the product that can be branded with different labels, associated with the producer/winery. For this reason, the brand name capital asset presents an average high degree of specificity. On the contrary, a "product" asset specificity is extremely high. In particular, the product name capital is protected with a particular label that adds to the producers' brand name. This implies that the investment in brand capital is not easily redeployed.

- TEMPORAL ASSETS

Temporal specificity is moderate, since Prosecco production and quality are characterized by a precise aging process that features the existence and the essence of the product.

Table 5.2 provides an assessment of the level of transaction costs that incur in the production and exchange of Prosecco. The indicators synthesize qualitatively the information.

D. Transaction costs minimizing governance structure: the Consortium

In synthesis, the potentially moderate opportunistic behavior, average complexity, average dedicated and human capital asset specificity, brand name, and high site asset specificity increase transaction costs. This implies and requires a certain degree of coordination in the organization of transactions, which cannot be completely performed in the markets. On the other hand, low/average levels of uncertainty and most types of asset specificities would not drive towards hierarchical structures.

In this framework, the Prosecco DOCG Consortium represents a transaction-cost-minimizing governance structure. The Consortium is a "hybrid" (Williamson, 1979) structure in which the degree of specificity of several investments and the uncertainty in the transactions' organizations are, with some exceptions, not particularly high. However, there are peculiar assets that present a high/very high degree of specificity. Moreover, the strict regulatory requirements that organize production and characterize input dramatically increase complexity. This generates the need for a

Table 5.2 Qualitative Assessment of TC for Prosecco

Behavioral Assumptions	
Bounded Rationality	Negligible
Opportunistic Behavior	Feasible
Variables Affecting Transaction Costs	
Uncertainty	Low/average
Complexity	Average
Asset Specificity	
Physical assets	Low specificity
Dedicated assets	Low/average specificity
Human assets	Average specificity
Site	High specificity
Brand name capital	Average/high specificity
Temporal	High/average specificity

certain degree of coordination in the organization of transactions, carried on in and by the Consortium that establishes and monitors the respect of the rules and instructions on quality standards through the Consortium protocol (*Disciplinare*). Coordination, in turn, is guaranteed by the existence and action of the Consortium that sets the rules for the selection of grapes providers and wine producers, the rules related to the definition of the product and its production and exchange conditions, and the rules related to quality requirements. In synthesis, the regulation through the consortium becomes the key to achieve economic efficiency (TC minimizing). This is illustrated in what follows. Recalling Equation (1) from Chapter 1,

$$\begin{aligned}&\textit{TC minimizing Governance Structure}\\&\quad = \min(\textit{TC}\ (\textit{uncertainty}\ (\bullet), \textit{complexity}\ (\bullet), \textit{asset specificity}\ (\bullet), \alpha))\end{aligned} \tag{1}$$

We can rewrite for the Prosecco DOCG case study that:

$$\begin{aligned}\textit{Consortium} = \min(&\textit{TC}\ (\textit{uncertainty}\ (K), \textit{complexity}\ (G,\alpha),\\&\textit{asset specificity}\ (F)))\end{aligned} \tag{2}$$

where the Consortium is the most efficient governance structure resulting from the minimization of transaction costs. In turn, transaction costs derive from the uncertainty that arises from a set of variables *K* (mostly linked to climatic unexpected events) and the complexity that arises from a set of variables *G* (representing regulation on all stages of production; the brand label and regulation of the selection of the grapes; the monitoring of the second fermentation stage). In the end, asset specificity depends on a set of variables *F* (representing product name capital and high site asset specificity, dedicated and human average asset specificity).

The variable α represents sustainability. In the case of Prosecco DOCG, sustainability requirements affect the complexity and contribute to increasing transaction costs. The organization and coordination of transactions within the Prosecco DOCG Consortium positively affect and implement sustainability requirements, mostly in the social dimension. In particular, the procedure for selecting and selling/purchasing the *Glera* grapes occurs between the Prosecco wine producers and the winegrowers, organized in cooperatives (see Onofri et al., 2016 for a detailed analysis of the organization of Prosecco production). The cooperatives of *Glera* grapes negotiate with the Consortium a higher price (even double or triple) per tons of grapes than the price practiced on the market. Such benefit must be counterbalanced by a cost. The conferred *Glera* grapes have to present very high-quality standards.[3] Those standards are more stringent than the one prescribed by the *Disciplinare*.[4] When purchasing *Glera* grapes from the cooperatives of *Glera* winegrowers, the Consortium is not only purchasing high-quality input of production but also contributing to social sustainability. Despite the "fame" of an inefficient, assistance-based institution, the winegrowers' cooperatives attempt to incorporate the values of social and cultural cohesion and competitiveness in the markets within the mission of the company. Social cohesion emerges in an attempt to provide a steady income to cooperative shareholders (through the Consortium purchasing the grapes produced by shareholders). The long-term stability of income to the cooperative members aims to minimize the risks and volatility of the exchange in free markets. Also, social cohesion involves the strengthening of territorial belonging and sharing, including relationships with local institutions.[5]

The requirement to organize and coordinate the production and the transactions in a Consortium achieves both economic efficiency through transaction costs' minimization and social sustainability.

5. Conclusion

The chapter has applied a qualitative TCE analysis to assess whether the Conegliano Valdobbiadene Prosecco DOCG is the most efficient governance structure that coordinates production stages to achieve high quality. The main findings show that the potentially moderate opportunistic behavior, average complexity, average dedicated and human capital asset specificity, brand name, and high site asset specificity increase transaction costs. This implies and requires a certain degree of coordination in the organization of transactions, which cannot be completely performed in the markets. On the other hand, low/average levels of uncertainty and most types of asset specificities would not drive towards hierarchical structures. Those rules dramatically increase ex-ante TC but are fundamental to clearly define the product identity, quality, and excellence. In this perspective, complexity is increased by the regulation of wine grapes' trade for the production of Prosecco DOCG. The Prosecco producers, adhering to the Consortium, can purchase wine grapes in the "free market" and/or from winegrowers' cooperatives. The latter product is much more costly than the *Glera* grapes traded in the market. However, the regulation and trade conditions force cooperatives to sell very high-quality *Glera* grapes. By purchasing from the cooperatives at a higher price, the Consortium purchases a very high-quality production input that guarantees a better wine. At the same time, the Consortium contributes to strengthen social cohesion by supporting the local grapes producers' cooperatives. The Consortium represents the most efficient, hybrid structure for coordinating and regulating transactions. By regulating the quality of wine grapes, the Consortium also preserves sustainability with an emphasis on social sustainability.

Fixing the concepts: selected questions

- Why is the Consortium the most TC-minimizing governance structure in the case of Prosecco DOCG?
- Why is the Consortium implementing social sustainability when minimizing transaction costs?
- How do the provisions regulating product quality affect social sustainability?
- Why "using the price mechanism" is costly?
- What is the role of dedicated and human asset specificity in determining the incidence of transaction costs in the case of Prosecco DOCG?

Notes

1 The "Conegliano Valdobbiadene – Prosecco" wines referred to in Article 1 upon release for consumption must meet the following characteristics: "Conegliano Valdobbiadene – Prosecco": color: more or less intense straw yellow, brilliant; aroma: vinous, characteristic with a light fruity scent; flavor: pleasantly bitter and rightly savory; minimum total alcoholic strength by volume: 10.50% vol; minimum total acidity: 4.5 g/l; minimum non-reducing extract: 14.0 g/l; Sparkling "Conegliano Valdobbiadene – Prosecco": color: more or less intense straw yellow, brilliant, with evident development of bubbles; aroma: pleasant and characteristic of fruity; flavor: fresh, harmonious, pleasantly sparkling, fruity; minimum total alcoholic strength by volume: 10.50% vol; minimum total acidity: 4.5 g/l; minimum sugar-free extract: 14.0 g/l.

2 www.prosecco.it/en/consortium/.

3 For instance, grapes affected by different diseases and spoiled by climatic agents like hailstorm, mold, or dryness are not purchased by the cooperative. Grapes must contain a precise level of acidity and sugar content. Grapes must be conferred keeping in mind the prescribed annual yields (proportional to the land hectares).

The grapes' harvest has to respect the timetable (day and hour) set by the winery. If this does not occur, the grapes are not purchased. Controls can be visual and technical. The grapes that are not accepted for prime rate winemaking can be bargained upon, case by case, and purchased for other purposes. Those shareholders that present a temporal path of virtuous behavior (in terms of conferment of grapes that reflect high-quality standard can be admitted in the Quality Club).

4 Article 4, paragraph 7 generally regulates the characteristics that wine grapes require. For the DOCG wines i.e. “Conegliano Valdobbiadene – Prosecco” the maximum yield of grapes per hectare in specialized cultivation must not exceed 13.00 tons, and the minimum natural alcohol content by volume of the grapes destined for vinification must be 9.50 vol. The grapes destined for the production of wines with denomination of origin “Conegliano Valdobbiadene–Prosecco” superior and semi-sparkling sparkling wine may have a minimum alcoholic strength by volume natural of 9.00% vol., provided that the destination of the grapes suitable for being processed is expressly indicated in the official cellar documents and the annual grape report. However, if unfavorable climatic conditions occur, the exemption referred to in Annex II may be granted, point C, paragraph 2 of EC Reg. no. 606/2009. For sparkling wines entitled to the term “Superiore di Cartizze”, as per art. 1, paragraph 2, the maximum yield of grapes per hectare in specialized cultivation must not exceed 12 tons, and the minimum natural alcohol content by volume of the grapes destined for vinification must be 9.50 vol. Even in exceptionally favorable years, the quantities of grapes per hectare to be allocated to production of wines with denomination of controlled and guaranteed origin “Conegliano Valdobbiadene–Prosecco must be reported within the above limits, as long as the production does not exceed 20% same limits. Without prejudice to other destinations permitted by current legislation, this product quota cannot in each case be destined for the production of wines with a typical geographical indication name of the Glera variety, or varietal sparkling wine, always with the name of the same variety. Furthermore, with reference always to the product referred to in the previous paragraph, the Veneto region, on motivated request from the consortium for the protection of this designation of origin and after hearing the interested trade organizations, with their provision to be issued every year during the period immediately preceding the harvest, it can establish further different uses/destinations of the aforementioned grapes.

5 Despite the mutual purpose, however, what emerged is a clear willingness of the cooperative winery to implement a strategy that valorizes the quality of the input, even at the costs of the punishment of the individual shareholder who deviates from the required standard. The quality parameter is the key variable of internal regulation and cooperative performance. There is a strong link between regulation of quality standards and impacts on the winery’s economic performance. In the case of the winery, achieving mutualism is paradoxically favored by the maximization of profits and the ability to do business, which Treviso cooperative wineries appear to do very efficiently (see Onofri et al., 2016).

References

Menard, C. (2004). The Economics of Hybrid Organizations. *Journal of Institutional and Theoretical Economics*, 160, 345–376.

Onofri, L., L. Barisan and V. Bostto. (2016). Rules, Organizational Structures and Economic Performance: The Case of Prosecco Cooperative Wineries in the Treviso Area (with L. Barisan and V. Boatto). *Rivista di Economia Agraria*, 1, 86–96.

Williamson, O. (1979). Transaction-Cost Economics: The Governance of Contractual Relations. *Journal of Law and Economics*, 22, 233–261.

6 The case of Amarone della Valpolicella wine

1. Introduction

The chapter applies the economic analysis presented in the first part of the book to the case of Amarone della Valpolicella wine production and organization. The chapter is organized as follows. Section 2 describes the product and describes the main production phases. Section 3 presents key figures on the Amarone wine market performance and production. Section 4 applies TCE analysis to show (1) why the production is managed and organized in a consortium, seen as an efficient transaction costs minimizing governance structure; and (2) how economic efficiency of the organization, food quality, and environmental sustainability can self-enforce and cause no trade-off in the case of Amarone della Valpolicella wine. Section 5 concludes the chapter.

2. The product

Amarone della Valpolicella is one of Italy's iconic wines. Valpolicella is the area where Amarone is made, and it lies north of Verona in northeast Italy, running 25 km from the Adige River in the west to Soave in the east. Amarone wine is strictly defined by the regulation (*Disciplinare*), which is established by the Amarone Wine Consortium. Article 1 of the regulation clearly states that the PDO label "Amarone della Valpolicella" is applied only to those wines that "*respond to the conditions and requirements set out in this production specification*".[1] Besides, Article 6 provides a detailed description of what the final product has to be like and what characteristics it has to present.[2]

The Consortium defines the boundaries and establishes what Amarone wine is on the grounds of three main criteria:

(1) the wine grape types and amount in the composition of the wine making (Article 2),[3]

(2) the extremely detailed delimitation of the geographical provenience of the wine (Article 3),[4] and
(3) the respect of the production steps and procedures (Articles 4 and 5).

The production of Amarone wine is laborious, costly, and articulated on complex stages. The most important grape varieties for Amarone production are Corvina, Corvinone, and Rondinella. Corvina is the most important variety of the grape blend for the production of Valpolicella wines, so that the regulations accept the use of such grapes between 45% and 95%. Rondinella variety, which is cold hardy and drought-resistant, can be used to between 5% and 30% (floral aromas and low tannin). Corvinone variety can form up to 50% of the grape blend, while other red varieties may be added to the blend with an overall maximum of 15% and 10% per single variety. The grapes have to be mostly cultivated according to a traditional, local method. This is the technique of the "*pergola Veronese*". This is a form of cultivation, dating back to Ancient Romans, in which the vegetative surface is laid out on a roof tilted slightly upwards of 20–30 degrees to the vertical pole. After hand harvest, Amarone grapes are dried in well-ventilated drying rooms (*fruttai*) with dehumidifiers to control temperature and humidity (from 60 to 120 days), they and must lose a minimum of 40% water content. Grapes must be dehydrated without heating. Grapes are pressed in the period of December–January and then fermented. Vinification of the grapes is not allowed before December 1. After vinification, it follows fermentation. Most producers ferment with natural yeast or prefer starting with it and finish with commercial yeast. Fermentations last from 2 to 6 weeks and are carried out in barrels; the fermentation can as long as 60 days to complete.

After the fermentation is complete, the wines are transferred into barrels made of oak or chestnut (traditional) and begin the aging process. Aging starts around a half-year after the harvest date. The minimum aging time is 25 months, and it is extended up to 50 months for Amarone Riserva.

3. Amarone wine-selected figures on product and market performance

Table 6.1 reports the main figures and facts related to Amarone della Valpolicella wine according to the available data. The purpose of the section is simply to be descriptive and informative, and it aims to provide a background for the analysis.

Table 6.1 is divided into three main parts. The first part provides selected information on the market structure (number of firms) and performance. The second part of the table lists the most important production inputs

Table 6.1 Selected Figures on Market Structure and Performance

Indicator	*Numeric Figure*	*Description*
Market Structure Indicators		
Wine Producers	2,347	Number of farms producing Amarone wine. They are not all belonging to the Consortium that regulates production and quality standards. They strictly follow the requirements contained in the Consortium regulation, since it is preliminary to having the authorization of labeling the wine as Amarone wine.
Domestic Demand	37% of production	Percentage distribution of demand. Domestic demand includes household and industrial—away from home consumption and food industry use.
International Demand	63% of production	Main importing countries: Germany and the United States
Selected Production Inputs		
Vineyard Land	8,030 hectares	Total extension of land destined to the production of Amarone wine grapes and recorded in the Valpolicella registers
Average Productivity of Vineyard Land	4 tons	Amount of wine grapes produced per hectare per year Regulated maximum grape yield is 12 tons/ha + 20%. Grapes for Amarone: max. 65% of the total allowed production
Average Productivity of Firms	6,348	Number of bottles produced by each firm.
Fruttai	431	Number of drying rooms for the drying of the grapes
Productivity of Wine Grapes	0.40 liters	From 1 kg of dried grapes suitable for making Amarone, 0.40 liters are obtained.

Indicator	*Numeric Figure*	*Description*
Economic Performance Main Indicators		
Output Quantity (Wine)	14.9 million	Number of bottles produced in 2018
Output Value (Wine)	600	Million Euro Revenues (2018)
Output Quantity (Grapes)	32,700	Tons of produced grapes for Amarone wine. However, a minimum of 3300 vines per hectare (excluding vineyards already belonging to the appellation and terraced vineyards with dry stone retention walls) are required by regulation.
Output Value (Grapes)	150	Million Euro (2018)
Price (Wine)	22	Euro per bottle, average price

Source: Our elaboration with data from Amarone Wine Consortium[5]

and productivity. The last part of the table provides information on recent economic performance, prices, produced quantity, and revenues. The figures are illustrative of an extremely positive economic performance that is increasing in time.

4. Transaction costs economic analysis of Amarone wine production

We will recall shortly the foundations of TCE theory, presented in Chapter 1. According to TCE, the most efficient governance structure, associated with industrial production including agri-food, is the one resulting from efficient transaction costs minimization. Transaction costs are the costs of running the economic system of firms (Williamson, 1979). The theory suggests that each type of transaction produces coordination costs of monitoring, controlling, and managing transactions. They mostly depend on three key variables: (1) uncertainty of the transaction, (2) complexity of the transaction, and (3) asset specificity required by the transaction. The degree of intensity of such variables affects the level (quantitatively or qualitatively quantified) of the transaction costs, which, in turn, define the most efficient governance structure. The higher the degree of asset specificity, uncertainty, and complexity of the transactions, the lower the reliance on the (neoclassical) market mechanism (that does not guarantee the minimization of transaction costs), and the higher the reliance on hybrid and hierarchical institutional structures (see Menard, 2004).

In what follows, qualitative TCE analysis is applied by describing the content of the variables required to, in our setting, qualitatively upraise the level of transaction costs in the production of Amarone della Valpolicella wine.

A. Behavioral assumptions

Bounded rationality

Bounded rationality implies that the economic agents cannot choose within all possible contingencies and situations since they are not familiar with them. In the case of the production of Amarone della Valpolicella, wine producers operate with a well-known technology in a stable environment with a stable demand worldwide. The consequences of bounded rationality may be limited.

Opportunistic behavior

Opportunistic behavior is defined as a condition of seeking self-interest with guile, including hidden information and hidden actions. In this way, it is expected that some agents behave differently from what they appear to be doing. According to this definition, it is possible to state that in the case of Amarone wine opportunistic behavior is partially limited by the direct observability of the performance and input of production and by the system of punishments for those who deviate from the regulation on quality standards, which incentivize credible commitment. In the case of Amarone della Valpolicella, however, the incentive to deviate from the strict regulation might be higher, since the costs of respecting such a stringent regulation might be very high and since the complex regulation requires higher frequency and intensity of controls.

B. Variables affecting transaction costs uncertainty

Uncertainty can be defined as imperfect knowledge about an event and its outcome. The highest degree of uncertainty, in this perspective, refers to problems that may arise during production and is related to harvesting uncertainty due to climate change and biotic and abiotic threats to grapes production. Another source of uncertainty refers to the possibility that the aging of the wine does not occur properly due to natural and/or processing causes. The latter implies negative effects on the quality and quantity of Amarone della Valpolicella wine and, in turn, on the pricing mechanism. Uncertainty is unlikely to dramatically affect the fluctuations of demand since the product is very well known by a niche segment of consumers with high reservation prices.

Complexity

Complexity refers to many different dimensions related to the implementation of the transaction. As far as frequency is concerned, it is extremely low, since the Amarone della Valpolicella wine is produced once per year. It represents a one-shot game. What increases the complexity of transactions and therefore dramatically increases transaction costs is the strict regulation (*Disciplinare*) that carefully indicates production steps and requirements. According to the *Disciplinare*, the following requirements are necessary (but not sufficient) conditions to label the product as Amarone della Valpolicella wine.

The first requirement demands that the Amarone grapes are harvested exclusively by hand. Mechanical harvesting is prohibited to preserve the quality and integrity of the grapes. Moreover, the cultivation technique based on the *pergola Veronese* system (that applies to 75% of total production) does not allow mechanical harvesting, which is a cheaper operation. The producers must indicate the vintage date and on the label. Moreover, the regulation induces low productivity of wine grapes since the yield of grapes into wine cannot exceed 40%. Usually, the grapes productivity for red wine is around 70%. This implies that from 1 kg of grapes destined to produce red wine, 0.70 liters of wine are obtained, while with 1 kg of dried grapes suitable for making Amarone della Valpolicella wine, only 0.40 liters are obtained.

The second requirement implies that drying is mandatory for at least 3 months. Only perfectly healthy grapes can survive the drying period unscathed. This requires that expert grape harvesters must carefully select the best grapes during the harvest to minimize losses. Only 65% of the harvest can be used for the production of Amarone. During drying, the weight loss of the grapes has to be included between 35 and 50%. This involves a significant decrease in production quantities, but it ensures an increase in quality due to the concentration of sugars, aromas, and polyphenols in the berries.

Amarone della Valpolicella is one of the few wines whose fermentation begins in winter due to withering, which is essential to make the grapes suitable for production. The low temperatures and the high amounts of sugars slow down or can even block fermentation, which must therefore be followed with particular care and expertise.

The productivity of land and wine grapes is strictly regulated as is the minimum alcohol content of the grapes before and after dehydration, the minimum alcohol content of the wine and all production phases, from harvesting to bottling that must mandatorily take place in the area of production except for the holders of a temporary or permanent authorization.

Such a detailed and stringent regulation not only increases production costs (for instance by requiring hand-harvesting that is more time and labor-consuming) but mostly increases transaction costs because it exacerbates the complexity of organization of transactions. This implies that the organization of the transactions is more costly at all production stages. This implies a constant monitoring activity that requires coordination and credible commitment and sanctionative power.

Asset specificity

There is the potential presence of different specific assets since the investments made to support a particular transaction have a higher value to that transaction than they would have if they were redeployed for any other objective. Asset specificity is a variable that refers to the characteristics of the investments that need to be done to make the product unique and which cannot be redeployed to alternative uses. The lower the asset specificity, the lower the transaction costs; while the higher the asset specificity, the higher the transaction costs. In the case of Amarone della Valpolicella wine, the different types of assets specificity are:

- PHYSICAL ASSETS

Physical assets are easily redeployable. Land and meadows can be used for other types of cultivations. Industrial machinery and plants easily are reused for the production of different wines. There is, therefore, a low level of physical asset specificity.

- DEDICATED ASSETS

Dedicated assets are linked to investment for building "pergola" and "fruttai" and purchase of particular barrels and barriques in oak and chestnut wood.

- HUMAN ASSETS

Human assets involved are weakly specific, with exception of specialized enologists.

- SITE ASSETS

Site specificity plays an important role because of regulation and contractual constraints. Amarone can only come from the Valpolicella area. Bottling must mandatorily take place in the area of production except for the holders of a temporary or permanent authorization.

- BRAND NAME CAPITAL

A brand signals a high-quality product to consumers. However, in the case of Amarone, the brand name refers to the product that can be branded with different labels, associated with the producer/winery. For this reason, the brand name capital asset presents an average high degree of specificity. On the contrary, a "product" asset specificity is extremely high.

- TEMPORAL ASSETS

Temporal specificity is high since Amarone production and quality are characterized by a precise aging process that features the existence and the essence of the product.

Table 6.2 provides an assessment of the level of transaction costs that incur in the production and exchange of Amarone della Valpolicella wine. The indicators synthesize qualitatively the information.

Table 6.2 Qualitative Assessment of TC for Amarone della Valpolicella

Behavioral Assumptions	
Bounded Rationality	Negligible
Opportunistic Behavior	Feasible
Variables Affecting Transaction Costs	
Uncertainty	Low/average
Complexity	High
Asset Specificity	
Physical assets	Low specificity
Dedicated asset	Average specificity
Human assets	Low specificity
Site	High specificity
Brand name capital	Average/high specificity
Temporal	High specificity

C. Transaction costs minimizing governance structure: the Consortium

In synthesis, the high complexity, temporal, and high site asset specificity increase transaction costs. This implies and requires a certain degree of coordination in the organization of transactions, which cannot be completely performed in the markets. On the other hand, low/average levels of uncertainty and most types of asset specificities would not drive towards hierarchical structures.

In this framework, the Consortium of Amarone della Valpolicella wine represents a transaction-cost-minimizing governance structure. The Consortium is a "hybrid" (Williamson, 1979) structure in which the degree of specificity of several investments and the uncertainty in the transactions' organizations are, with some exceptions, not particularly high. However, there are peculiar assets that present a high/very high degree of specificity. Moreover, the strict regulatory requirements that organize production and characterize input dramatically increase complexity. This generates the need for a certain degree of coordination in the organization of transactions, carried on in and by the Consortium that establishes and monitors the respect of the rules and instructions on quality standards through the Consortium protocol (*Disciplinare*). According to the set of complex rules, Amarone della Valpolicella wine is only recognized and labeled as that wine that is produced in accordance with *Disciplinare* rules and is recognized ex-post, through the Consortium accreditation, upon controls. Only when all complex stages are fulfilled and controlled, the winery is allowed to name its product as Amarone della Valpolicella wine. The strengthening of regulatory requirements "in the making" allows to market a well-identified and well-recognizable product, whose identity, quality, and excellency are defined and guaranteed by the regulation and coordinated production. Coordination, in turn, is guaranteed by the existence and action of the Consortium that sets the rules for the selection of wine grape—the rules related to the definition of the product and its production and exchange conditions and the rules related to quality requirements. In synthesis, the regulation through the Consortium becomes the key to achieve economic efficiency (TC minimizing). This is illustrated in what follows. Recalling Equation (1) from Chapter 1,

$$\textit{TC minimizing Governance Structure} = \min(\textit{TC}\ (\textit{uncertainty}\ (\bullet), \textit{complexity}\ (\bullet), \textit{asset specificity}\ (\bullet), \alpha)) \quad (1)$$

We can rewrite for the Amarone della Valpolicella case study that:

$$\textit{Consortium} = \min(\textit{TC}\ (\textit{uncertainty}\ (K), \textit{complexity}\ (G,\alpha), \textit{asset specificity}\ (F))) \quad (2)$$

where the Consortium is the most efficient governance structure resulting from the minimization of transaction costs. In turn, transaction costs derive from uncertainty arisen from a set of variables K (climate change, abiotic and biotic threats, wine aging). *TC* is generated by the complexity that arises from a set of variables G (representing strict regulation on all stages of production). In the end, asset specificity depends on a set of variables F (representing product name capital, temporal, and high site asset specificity).

Moreover, the variable α represents sustainability. In the case of Amarone della Valpolicella, sustainability requirements affect the complexity and contribute to increasing transaction costs. The organization and coordination of transactions within Amarone della Valpolicella Consortium, however, positively affect and implement sustainability requirements, mostly in the environmental dimension. Environmental sustainability is a key factor in food quality and security. The *Disciplinare* sets very stringent rules on the use of defense against biotic and abiotic threats, with an emphasis on limitations and rationed applications. For instance, the *Disciplinare* regulates the frequency of treatments against downy mildew. Those treatments cannot be undertaken more than three times per year with the same active principle and no more than five times with different active principles. The *Disciplinare* even lists the allowed active principle and provided indications on the dosage (max 5 kilos per ha) and strict limitations (e.g., on the use of copper). Similar dispositions apply for powdery mildew (three treatments per year) and botrytis (1 treatment per year).

In this perspective, the sustainability indicators are mostly of the environmental dimension type and signal an attempt to preserve the natural capital and natural production inputs (land, water, and wine grapes). Those provisions can be interpreted as rules that not only define the quality requirements for production inputs but also environmental sustainability standards. Those rules are strictly implemented even if they might turn in costly losses and in a higher risk of production, since reducing the number and aggressivity of treatments against biotic and abiotic threats might increase the risk of losses of wine grapes. The requirement to organize and coordinate the production and the transactions in a Consortium allows to achieve both economic efficiency through transaction costs minimization and environmental sustainability.

5. Conclusion

The chapter has applied a qualitative TCE analysis in order to assess whether the Amarone della Valpolicella wine Consortium is the most efficient governance structure. Besides, through the definition, implementation, and strict monitoring of rules, the Consortium coordinates production and commercialization and secures ex-ante specific investment in brand capital value, which in this case is declined in the case of "product capital value", since the Amarone Wine can be branded with different labels carrying the name of the producers. The high degree of complexity is generated by stringent rules set in the *Disciplinare*. Those rules dramatically increase ex ante TC but are fundamental to clearly define the product identity, quality, and excellency.

The main findings show that the degree of complexity/frequency, brand name, and site asset specificity that affects the level of TC is mostly linked to the "unicity" of the product and the requirement to keep the quality standards. Moreover, the regulation on quality standards increases TC, through a complexity increase for the sake of defining the unicity and idiosyncrasy of the product. This affects the TC and the related organization of the transactions. The Consortium represents the most efficient, hybrid structure for coordinating and regulating transaction costs (in the case at issue mostly generated by complexity). By regulating the product identity and quality, the Consortium also preserves sustainability with an emphasis of environmental sustainability that is pursued even at the cost of increasing production risks.

Fixing the concepts: selected questions

- Why is the Consortium the most TC-minimizing governance structure in the case of Amarone della Valpolicella wine?
- Why is the Consortium implementing environmental sustainability when minimizing transaction costs?
- How do the provisions regulating the product quality affect environmental sustainability?

- Why "using the price mechanism" is costly?
- Which key variables mostly affect the degree of transaction costs in the case of Amarone della Valpolicella wine? In particular, why is complexity dramatically increasing transaction costs?

Notes

1 The controlled and guaranteed designation of origin "Amarone della Valpolicella", already recognized as a typology with DPR August 21, 1968, is reserved for wines that respond to the conditions and requirements set out in this production specification, for the following types: "Amarone della Valpolicella" can also be designated with the references "classic" and "Valpantena" and with the specification "reserve".

2 The wine with a controlled and guaranteed designation of origin "Amarone della Valpolicella" and with the references "classic" and "Valpantena" and with the specification "reserve" must meet the following characteristics at the release for consumption: (1) color: red load tending, where appropriate, to garnet, as it ages; (2) odor: characteristic, accentuated; (3) flavor: full, velvety, warm; (4) minimum effective alcoholic strength by volume: 14% vol.; (5) total maximum residual sugars: 9 g/l in the presence of actual alcoholic strength of 14% vol.; an additional 0.1 g/l of residual sugars per 0.10% vol. of alcoholic strength more than 14% vol. and up to 16% vol., and 0.15 g/l of residual sugars for every 0.10% vol. of actual alcoholic strength over 16% vol; (6) minimum total acidity: 5.0 g/l; (7) minimum nonreducing extract: 28.0 g/l and 32.0 g/l in the "reserve" version.

3 The wines of the controlled and guaranteed designation of origin "Amarone della Valpolicella" must be obtained from the grapes produced by the vineyards having, within the company, the following ampelographic composition: (1) Corvina Veronese (Cruina or Corvina) and/or Corvinone from 45% to 95% and (2) Rondinella from 5% to 30%. They can contribute to the production of these wines, up to a maximum of 25% of the total grapes from the vines: (1) nonaromatic red berry, allowing for the cultivation in the province of Verona referred to in the National Register of Vine Varieties approved by Decree of May 7, 2004 (OJ No 242, October 14, 2004) and subsequent updates, up to a maximum of 15% with a maximum of 10% for each grape variety used; (2) classified native Italian according to law no. 238/2016, Article 6, red berry, allowed cultivation for the Province of Verona referred to in the National Register of Vine Varieties approved by decree of May 7, 2004 (OJ No 242 of October 14, 2004) and subsequent updates, for the remaining quantity of 10% total.

4 Article 3 provides a detailed (4 pages) list of the allowed geographical areas.

5 www.consorziovalpolicella.it.

References

Menard, C. (2004). The Economics of Hybrid Organizations. *Journal of Institutional and Theoretical Economics*, 160, 345–376.

Williamson, O. (1979). Transaction-Cost Economics: The Governance of Contractual Relations. *Journal of Law and Economics*, 22, 233–261.

7 The case of Prosciutto di San Daniele del Friuli

1. Introduction

The chapter applies the economic analysis presented in the first part of the book to the case Prosciutto di San Daniele production and organization. The chapter is organized as follows. Section 2 provides a description of the product and the main production phases. Section 3 presents key figures on Prosciutto di San Daniele market performance. Section 4 applies TCE analysis in order to show (1) why the production is managed and organized in a consortium, seen as an efficient transaction costs minimizing governance structure and (2) how economic efficiency of the organization, food quality, and environmental sustainability can self-enforce and cause no trade-off in the case of Prosciutto di San Daniele. Section 5 concludes the chapter.

2. The product

Prosciutto di San Daniele del Friuli is a typical ham, being produced in the same way for centuries in the village of San Daniele del Friuli in the North East of Italy.

It is an Italian product of excellence with deep roots in the place where it is produced and characterized by climate conditions (winds that blow from the Carnic Alps to the Adriatic) that confer a very peculiar and unmistakable fragrance and flavor to the final product.

Article 3, paragraph 1 of the Production Regulation (*Disciplinare*) defines Prosciutto di San Daniele as:

> characterized by its external guitar shape including the distal part (foot). The weight of whole Prosciutto di San Daniele on the bone is usually between 8 and 10 kg and in any case never less than 7.5 kg. The meat is compact, tender, and elastic with the fat part perfectly white, in the right proportion with the lean portion of pink and red color with some streaks of fat. The taste is delicately sweet with a more pronounced

aftertaste. The aroma is fragrant and characteristic depending on the seasoning period.

The product is described in a very detailed way by the provisions set in the *Disciplinare*.[1]

The production stages are organized and articulated as follows. San Daniele is made only with pigs born, raised, and slaughtered exclusively in Italy. They are fed a controlled diet based on whey and high-quality grain as set out in the *Disciplinare*. The fresh pork legs are delivered from the authorized abattoir directly to the production plant and are subjected to preliminary compliance checks to ensure that they come from authorized abattoirs. Only legs of pork that pass this stage are then allowed to begin with the preparation and curing process. The selected meats are kept for 24 hours at a temperature between −1°C and + 3°C to "tone up". In the end, they are trimmed with specially chosen cuts to encourage moisture loss. Twenty-four hours later, the legs are covered with sea salt and hung at a temperature between 0° and 4°C. Maturation is strictly restricted to within the municipality of San Daniele del Friuli. According to the tradition, each ham rests in this state for a period based on its weight, with one day for each kilogram of weight. This process allows the leg to be preserved naturally while maintaining the integrity of the meat and improving its flavor. After salting, the legs are pressed along the muscle mass to allow the salt to penetrate deeply and give the meat an optimal consistency for the maturing process. Exclusive to San Daniele ham, this procedure gives it the characteristic guitar shape. The salted legs rest in special rooms, where the humidity is kept between 70% and 80% and the temperature between 4°C and 6°C. This phase continues until the fourth month after the start of processing, which allows the salt to penetrate uniformly and become evenly distributed within the meat. Maturation takes 13 months after processing. It is essential to maintain optimum temperature, humidity, and ventilation conditions during the entire maturing process. The surface of the exposed, rind-free part of the prosciutto undergoes a process called "*sugnatura*" or smearing. This involves smearing the exposed meat with a paste made of lard and rice or wheat flour to protect and soften that part of the prosciutto and prevent the meat underneath from drying out. As the ham matures, it needs to be repeatedly checked to see how the process is progressing. This is done by regularly testing every leg. Two types of tests are carried out: striking the leg to check the firmness of the ham and pricking it with a horse-bone needle in specific points on the leg and smelling the ham's aroma to assess the meat's quality and how it is maturing. The quality control body IFCQ *Certificazioni Srl* performs the final checks on the prosciutto only after the end of the thirteenth month. The independent control body IFCQ is supervised by the

Italian Ministry of Agriculture, Food and Forestry Policies and accredited by the National Accreditation Authority designated by the Italian government. Only the hams that pass these tests can be certified and branded with the San Daniele mark, which includes the producer's identification code and guarantees the quality of the product.

3. Prosciutto di San Daniele-selected figures on product and market performance

Table 7.1 reports the main figures and facts related to the Prosciutto di San Daniele market performance. The data were recorded in 2019. The purpose of the section is simply descriptive and aims to provide a background for the analysis.

Table 7.1 Selected Figures on Market Structure and Performance

Indicator	*Numeric Figure*	*Description*
Market Structure Indicators		
Authorized Farms	3,851	Number of farms selected and authorized by the Consortium in 10 different Italian regions to breed pigs for Prosciutto di San Daniele
Abattoirs	54	Number of abattoirs authorized to process pigs
Producers	31	Number of ham producers in the village of San Daniele
Slicing Facilities	9	Number of slicing and packaging facilities in the village of San Daniele
Domestic Demand	82% of production	Percentage distribution of demand. Domestic demand includes household and industrial—away from home consumption and food industry use
International Demand	18% of production	55% to EU countries, 45% to non-EU countries (mostly Canada and Japan)
Economic Performance Main Indicators		
Output Quantity	21.2 million	Certified packs of pre-sliced product
	2.5 million	Units of prosciutto (legs)
Output Value	310	Million euro revenues (2019)
Price	30	Euro per kilo, average price
	42	Euro per kilo for the sliced pre-packaged product

Source: Our elaboration with data from Prosciutto di San Daniele Consortium[2]

Table 7.1 is divided into two parts. The first part provides selected information on the market structure (number of farms and producers) and performance. The second part of the table provides information on recent economic performance, prices, produced quantities, and revenues. The figures are illustrative of an extremely positive economic performance that is increasing in time.

4. Transaction costs economic analysis of Prosciutto di San Daniele del Friuli

We recall shortly the foundations of TCE theory as presented in Chapter 1. According to TCE, the most efficient governance structure, associated with industrial production, including agri-food, is the one resulting from efficient transaction costs minimization. Transaction costs are the costs of running the economic system of firms (Williamson, 1979). The theory suggests that each type of transaction produces coordination costs of monitoring, controlling, and managing transactions. They mostly depend on three key variables: (1) uncertainty of the transaction, (2) complexity of the transaction, and (3) asset specificity required by the transaction. The degree of intensity of such variables affects the level (quantitatively or qualitatively quantified) of the transaction costs, which, in turn, define the most efficient governance structure. The higher the degree of asset specificity, uncertainty, and complexity of the transactions, the lower the reliance on the (neoclassical) market mechanism (that does not guarantee the minimization of transaction costs), and the higher the reliance on hybrid and hierarchical institutional structures (see Menard, 2004).

In what follows, qualitative TCE analysis is applied by describing the content of the variables required to, in our setting, qualitatively upraise the level of transaction costs in the production of Prosciutto di San Daniele.

A. Behavioral assumptions

Bounded rationality

Bounded rationality implies that the economic agents cannot choose within all possible contingencies and situations since they are not familiar with all of them. In the case of Prosciutto di San Daniele, producers operate with a well-known technology in a stable environment with a stable demand worldwide. Besides, some contingencies can be forecasted thanks to the millenary production of this product that has allowed the accumulation of traditional knowledge capital, based on empirical experience. The consequences of bounded rationality may be limited.

Opportunistic behavior

Opportunistic behavior is defined as a condition of seeking self-interest with guile, including hidden information and hidden actions. In this way, it is expected that some agents behave differently from what they appear to be doing. According to this definition, it is possible to state that in the case of Prosciutto di San Daniele, opportunistic behavior is limited by the direct observability of the production performance that can only take place in the village of San Daniele del Friuli and by the selection rules of the factors of production. Besides, the system of punishments (synthesized in an Ethical Code) for those who deviate from the regulation on quality standards incentivize credible commitment. In this perspective, opportunistic behavior may be negligible.

B. Variables affecting transaction costs

Uncertainty

Uncertainty can be defined as imperfect knowledge about an event and its outcome. The highest degree of uncertainty in this perspective refers to problems that may arise during production and is related to the possibility that the aging of the hams does not occur properly due to natural and/or processing causes. The latter implies the impossibility to brand and commercialize the ham as Prosciutto di San Daniele. This, in turn, may affect supply price and quantity. Another source of uncertainty refers to the search for quality inputs (pigs) and the monitoring of the final output quality standards (which are observable in time) and therefore moderate. Uncertainty may also negatively affect the fluctuations of demand. Fluctuations in demand are limited in markets where the product is well known. Fluctuations in demand are subject to large variances in markets where the product is not well known and it competes with (potential, perceived) substitutes that are evaluated by the consumers only on a price basis. In this perspective, differently than Parmigiano Reggiano, which is more well known, Prosciutto di San Daniele is exported worldwide at extremely expensive prices for a small niche of consumers. This exposes to a large uncertainty on demand fluctuations. Informed consumers are aware of the intrinsic unique, qualitative differences between the products. Uninformed consumers are not aware of it. The informational asymmetry may increase transaction uncertainty in those markets. This requires a certain degree of organizational coordination that is implemented through formation, R&D, education, certification, and continuous monitoring. The need to communicate and spread information on the unicity of the product has spurred the Consortium to invest in research and training activities in collaboration with relevant organizations as well as support development in the scientific and cultural fields and to organize educational, information-based, and product promotion initiatives that are dedicated to the communities in Italy and abroad.

Complexity

Complexity refers to many different dimensions related to the implementation of the transaction. Among those there is the transaction frequency, that is, the number of times the transaction is expected to take place is high. The frequency of transactions is high. The production phases do not involve high complexity. Besides, the requirements to guarantee the high-quality standards of inputs and outputs and to keep the level of the Prosciutto di San Daniele ham reputation call for the adoption of an effective certification mechanism—the definition and implementation of strategies aiming at monitoring, communicating, and legally protecting the reputation. Before that, it is also important to get the product known and to highlight the product's main (qualitative and intrinsic) differences from other types of Italian hams. The Prosciutto di San Daniele Consortium, for instance, has established both a digital traceability system and a rigorous and certified system of product identification along its value chain, which extends right up to the application of the certified PDO branding.[3] The Consortium continuously monitors for abuses or illegal use of the trademark or Protected Designation of Origin (PDO) worldwide both during the product marketing stage and online, where it is checked for any misuse of Internet domains that are identical or similar to "Prosciutto di San Daniele".[4]

The high frequency of the exchanges and the need to communicate, educate, and preserve the high reputation of the product worldwide increase complexity and require a certain degree of coordination of the transactions.

Asset specificity

There is the potential presence of different specific assets since the investments made to support a particular transaction have a higher value to that transaction than they would have if they were redeployed for any other objective. Asset specificity is a variable that refers to the characteristics of the investments that need to be done to make the product unique and which cannot be redeployed to alternative uses. The lower the asset specificity the lower the transaction costs; while the higher the asset specificity the higher the transaction costs. In the case of Prosciutto di San Daniele, the different types of asset specificity are:

- PHYSICAL ASSETS

Physical assets can be redeployable. Industrial machinery and plants for ham production can easily be reused for the production of different cured meats. There is, therefore, a low level of physical asset specificity.

- DEDICATED ASSETS

Dedicated assets are limited.

- HUMAN ASSETS

Human assets involved are weekly specific, even if producers and "*mastri prosciuttai*" (ham experts) might have accumulated a knowledge capital and expertise related to the monitoring of the product during the production stages, which may be lost if the production of Prosciutto di San Daniele stopped.

- SITE ASSETS

Site specificity plays an important role because of regulation and contractual constraints. In fact, only the prosciutto aged in the village of San Daniele del Friuli can be labeled as Prosciutto di San Daniele.

- BRAND NAME CAPITAL

The Prosciutto di San Daniele brand signals a high-quality product to consumers, thus reducing their uncertainty related to information searching and quality guarantee on the product characteristics, like proper aging and nutritional content. It also conveys a clear message on the whole idiosyncratic production procedure linked to product-specific expertise, history, and tradition.

The latter is highly idiosyncratic, and therefore the brand name capital asset presents a very high degree of specificity. Also, in this case, the brand signals a high-quality product to consumers. The brand name refers to both the product and the label (even if producers can also label with the name of the firm). For this reason, there is a high degree of the brand and product name capital specificity.

- TEMPORAL ASSETS

Temporal specificity is moderately low, given the high and repeated frequency of production.

Table 7.2 Qualitative Assessment of TC for Prosciutto di San Daniele

Behavioral Assumptions	
Bounded Rationality	Negligible
Opportunistic Behavior	Negligible
Variables Affecting Transaction Costs	
Uncertainty	Average/high
Complexity	Average
Asset Specificity	
Physical assets	Low specificity
Dedicated asset	Low specificity
Human assets	Low/average specificity
Site	Very high specificity
Brand name capital	High specificity
Temporal	Low specificity

Table 7.2 provides a qualitative assessment of the level of transaction costs that incur in the production and exchange of Prosciutto di San Daniele.

C. Transaction costs minimizing governance structure: the Consortium

In synthesis, uncertainty, brand/product name capital, and site asset specificity increase transaction costs. This implies and requires a certain degree of coordination in the organization of transactions, which cannot be completely performed in the markets. On the other hand, low/average levels of complexity and most types of asset specificities would not drive towards hierarchical structures.

In this framework, the Prosciutto di San Daniele Consortium represents a transaction-cost-minimizing governance structure. The Consortium is a "hybrid" (Williamson, 1979) structure in which the degree of specificity of several investments and complexity in the transactions' organizations are, with some exceptions, not particularly high. However, there are peculiar assets that present a high/very high degree of specificity and average-to-low degrees of uncertainty. This requires coordination in the organization of transactions, carried on in and by the Prosciutto di San Daniele Consortium that establishes and monitors the compliance the rules aiming to guarantee the quality standards through the Consortium *Disciplinare*.

Coordination is guaranteed by the existence and action of the Consortium that sets the rules for the selection of production inputs (pigs) and production stages, in particular requiring that hams (produced in authorized farms in the Italian territory) complete the aging process in the village of San Daniele under the supervision of skilled "*mastri prosciuttai*" who have accumulated expertise that has a millenary tradition. Also, the regulation defines what the product is and what the production and exchange conditions must be and the rules related to quality requirements. In the end, the Consortium coordinates and engages in effective education campaigns, whose objective encompasses product quality communications and focuses on transmitting information on the product per se. In synthesis, the regulation through the consortium becomes the key to achieve economic efficiency (TC minimizing) and, in turn, sustainability. This is illustrated in what follows.

Recalling Equation (1) from Chapter 1,

$$\begin{aligned}&\textit{TC minimizing Governance Structure}\\&\quad = \min(\textit{TC}\ (\textit{uncertainty}\ (\bullet), \textit{complexity}\ (\bullet), \textit{asset specificity}\ (\bullet), \alpha)) \qquad (1)\end{aligned}$$

We can rewrite for the Prosciutto di San Daniele case study that:

$$\begin{aligned}\textit{Consortium} = \min(&\textit{TC}\ (\textit{uncertainty}\ (K,\alpha), \textit{complexity}\ (G),\\&\textit{asset specificity}\ (F))) \qquad (2)\end{aligned}$$

where the Consortium is the most efficient governance structure resulting from the minimization of transaction costs. In turn, transaction costs are derived from uncertainty arisen from a set of variables K (representing markets with asymmetric information about the product "definition" and quality standards, aging of ham). TC is also generated by the complexity that arises from a set of variables G (representing certification—monitoring of reputation and respect of quality standards, digital traceability system, R&D, education on the product characteristics). In the end, asset specificity depends on a set of variables F (representing product/brand name capital and high site asset specificity).

The variable α represents sustainability. Sustainability requirements affect uncertainty and increase transaction costs. The organization and coordination of transactions within the Parmigiano Reggiano Consortium, however, aiming at minimizing TC through quality regulation positively affects and implements sustainability requirements, mostly in the economic and environmental sustainability dimension.

The strictly environmental sustainable dimension relies on a set of practices and provisions related to animal welfare in the selection and breeding of pigs, including a careful regulation of pigs' food and nutritional standards. Such rules activities are sustainable and environmental-friendly. They are also quality-oriented and aiming at improving the quality of the main production inputs, which, in turn, improves the quality of the final output.

Other practices embody both the environmental and economic dimensions of sustainability. The Consortium implements a plethora of activities aiming at supporting and assisting producers in the management of different "green" services, which span from wastewater disposal (288,402 m^3 of wastewater managed in 2019 through the consortium treatment plant) to efficient waste management (including the recovery of brine and solid salt). Consortium members recovered 3,673 tons of used solid salt, which was then used for other purposes such as the deicing of roads or in the tanning industry to collective management of electricity and gas services to maximize energy efficiency and minimize CO_2 emissions. Such activities are not directly involved in increasing the quality of the product per se but are involved in making production more green, circular, efficient, and, therefore, sustainable from the economic perspective.

The Consortium coordination activities achieve both economic efficiency and environmental and economic sustainability through transaction costs minimization.

5. Conclusion

The chapter has applied a qualitative TCE analysis to assess whether the Prosciutto di San Daniele del Friuli Consortium is the most efficient governance structure. The main findings show that the degree of uncertainty (due to the characteristic of niche product of Prosciutto di San Daniele and the high level of asymmetric information among consumers), the brand name (product brand name), and site asset specificity that affects the level of TC is mostly linked to the "unicity" of the product and the requirement to keep the quality standards. Moreover, the regulation on quality standards increases TC, through a complexity increase, for the sake of defining the unicity and idiosyncrasy of the product. This affects the TC and the related organization of the transactions. Through the definition, implementation, and strict monitoring of rules, the Consortium coordinates production and commercialization and represents the most efficient, hybrid structure for coordinating and regulating transaction costs (in the case at issue mostly generated by complexity). By regulating the product identity and quality, the Consortium also preserves sustainability with an emphasis on environmental and economic sustainability.

Fixing the concepts: selected questions

- Why is the Consortium the most TC-minimizing governance structure in the case of Prosciutto di San Daniele?
- Why is the Consortium implementing environmental sustainability when minimizing transaction costs?
- How do the provisions regulating the product quality affect environmental sustainability?

- Why "using the price mechanism" is costly?
- Which key variables mostly affect the degree of transaction costs in the case of Prosciutto di San Daniele? In particular, why is site specificity dramatically increasing transaction costs?

Notes

1 According to Article 3, Prosciutto di San Daniele is characterized by the following chemical parameters: Humidity must not be lower than 57%, nor higher than 63%. The quotient of the ratio between the percentage composition of sodium chloride and the percentage humidity must not be lower than 7.8 or higher than 11.2. The quotient of the ratio between the percentage humidity and the percentage composition in total proteins must not be lower than 1.9 nor higher than 2.5. The proteolysis index (percentage composition of the nitrogenous fractions soluble in trichloroacetic acid—TCA—referred to the of total nitrogen) must not exceed 31. The chemical parameters given before refer to the centesimal composition of a fraction of the hamstring muscle and are detected before affixing the mark. Prosciutto di San Daniele can also be released for consumption deboned, portioned that is divided into slices of variable shape and weight, or sliced. The mark is present in all types of products. Article 3.3—Raw materials (only for processed products): Live animals for the production of Prosciutto di San Daniele: Animals, in purity or derivatives, of the traditional Large White and Landrace basic breeds, as improved by the Italian Herd Book, are allowed. Animals derived from the Duroc breed are also allowed, as improved by the Italian Herd Book. Animals of other breeds, mestizos, and hybrids are also admitted, as long as they come from selection or crossing schemes implemented with purposes that are not incompatible with those of the Italian Herd Book for the production of heavy pigs. In compliance with tradition, carriers of antithetical characters are however excluded, with particular reference to sensitivity to stress (PSS). Pure breed animals of the Belgian Landrace, Hampshire, Pietrain, Duroc, and Spotted Poland breeds are excluded. The use of boars and sows is excluded. The genetic types used must ensure the achievement of high weights with good efficiencies and, in any case, an average weight per batch (live weight) of 160 kilograms plus or minus 10%. Fresh legs: The legs of pigs used for the preparation of Prosciutto di San Daniele, coming from heavy pig carcasses belonging to the 'U', 'R', 'O' classes of the Union table for the classification of pig carcasses, must be weighing no less than 11 kg. The thickness of the fat of the external part of the fresh trimmed thigh, measured vertically in correspondence of the femur, with the thigh and its external face placed on the horizontal plane, must not be less than 15 mm including the rind, depending on the size. Thighs from pigs with overt myopathies and evident sequelae from previous inflammatory and traumatic processes are excluded. The processing of pork legs that are obtained from pigs that have been slaughtered for less than 24 hours or more than 120 hours or that are frozen is not allowed. Article 3.4—Food for animals (only for products of animal origin): Detailed rules on the use and composition of the food must be observed. The food should preferably be presented in liquid form (broth or mash) and traditionally with whey. Article 3.5—Specific stages of production that must take place in the defined geographical area: All the processing stages of Prosciutto di San Daniele starting from the

trimming of the fresh legs up to the end of the curing period must take place within the Municipality of San Daniele del Friuli in the province of Udine. Article 3.6—Specific rules on slicing, grating, packaging, etc.: The packaging operations of the sliced product are carried out exclusively in the geographical area where the San Daniele ham is processed. Article 3.7—Specific rules on labeling: Specific rules are laid down for Prosciutto di San Daniele regarding the identification of the product, both in the context of the production circuit (raw material) and at the time of its final preparation and at the time of presentation in the commercial phase. In the context of the San Daniele Ham production circuit, the following sequence of identifying elements of the product is envisaged: stamp (s) affixed by the farmer, identification stamp of the slaughterhouse affixed by the butcher on the fresh legs, seal affixed by the care of the producer on fresh legs, conformity marking—brand—affixed to the rind of the ham under the responsibility and in the presence of the inspection body. The labeling of whole San Daniele ham with bone bears the following mandatory information: "Prosciutto di San Daniele", followed by "protected designation of origin", the location of the production plant. The labeling of whole boned Prosciutto di San Daniele, or presented in slices and sliced, must bear the following mandatory information: "Prosciutto di San Daniele", followed by "protected designation of origin", the location of the packaging plant, the production date (start of processing) in all cases in which the seal is no longer visible. The packs of sliced packaged San Daniele Ham must include the graphic reproduction of the mark and the indication of the packer's numeric identification code. The mark reproduces the one affixed to the rind of cured ham.

2 https://prosciuttosandaniele.it/.

3 The Consortium has implemented a digital traceability system that provides information in real time to guarantee the origin of the raw materials at every processing stage from livestock farming until final stages of production, starting from the 30th day of birth of the pork, when farmers must brand both thighs of the piglet with an indelible ink stamp; this is the farm's unique identification code.

4 There are three types of monitoring activities: (1) Ordinary monitoring activities (at retail and wholesale stores) and sample the product to ensure that it meets the requirements outlined in the *Disciplinare*. (2) Reporting-based monitoring activities (verification of commercial activities following reports received about price or quality anomalies. (3) Online monitoring activities, aiming at monitoring (we monitor the web to identify any misuse of the denomination or trademark in terms of both sales, promotion, and advertising).

References

Menard, C. (2004). The Economics of Hybrid Organizations. *Journal of Institutional and Theoretical Economics*, 160, 345–376.

Williamson, O. (1979). Transaction-Cost Economics: The Governance of Contractual Relations. *Journal of Law and Economics*, 22, 233–261.

8 Conclusion

1. Introduction

National and international (mostly EU) policies have recently aimed at enhancing the quality of food production, creating a turning point in perspectives that have gradually changed towards an all-encompassing action of global enhancement of the environment and sustainable values. This goes hand in hand with the general and widespread environmental awareness that is also appearing in Italy, after having become widespread in other countries and after being urged by international organizations and fora. Typical Italian agri-food products have aroused interest in their rediscovery. The institution of brands connotes not only the types of raw materials and the processing of maturation but also the places of origin, ranging from the PDO brand to the PGI. A final form of characterization can be seen in the idea of "traceability", which consists of identifying all the geographical and labor paths that underlie its formulation in the final product. A real complex of actions that leads to the recognition of a food product as a "treasure chest" that doubly connotes those who own it and those who seek it, not only for its economic value but also for its historical–cultural value. The culinary richness is highlighted as the sum of different forms of culture that are objectified in natural productions, enriched by expert and consolidated processes that testify the territory, the climate, and the ability to work. Appreciating the value of typical products, the value of tradition, craftsmanship, the richness of the soil and culture means recognizing them as an enriching heritage of our personality. Often these productions derive from very ancient recipes, preserved by a few experts and amateurs, and produced on an artisanal level, to which tourism ensures a source of supply. Typical products help to enhance the image of the entire production area and stimulate a growing flow of tourism aimed at increasing the economic value of tertiary and integrated agriculture.

The agricultural and agro-industrial question is no longer linked to quantitative production and its mere processing and marketing. There emerges a need to evaluate agri-food production agriculture and related extra-agricultural activities in their relationship with society and with the economic fabric that exists on the territory where production takes place. The agri-food sector not only produces goods that are not purely economic, but also produces the environment, tourism, and culture and necessarily implements activities that are linked with others in the areas of crafts and small and medium-sized enterprises. The key element of the sustainable enhancement strategy aims at a differentiated evolution of the different agricultural realities and a virtuous integration between environmental protection and socioeconomic development. For this reason, the ultimate goal is to “increase the competitiveness of businesses, maintaining the cohesion and integration of the socio-economic systems of the territory, favoring the protection of environmental resources”. In this new perspective, sustainability implies the integration of the policies of the economic sectors and environmental protection and becomes the engine of innovation and well-being. Integration of sustainability in production, thus, represents a developmental conceptual matrix of the agri-food sector and helps to achieve the enhancement of the quality of primary production, which addresses the need for a qualitative increase in food production that has globally achieved, even if not fairly, food sufficiency.

2. From high quality to high excellence: sustainability key

With several high-excellence food and wine products, the enhancement of the immense heritage represented by agri-food productions comes into play, typical expressions of the extreme variety of territories and local cultures of Italy, which have distinct distinctive characteristics that make them known and appreciated throughout the world. The sustainability matrix, advocated for quality agri-food production in general, finds a “natural” implementation avenue with high-excellence products.

The book has applied the theoretical framework of transaction costs economic (TCE) for analyzing the organization of high-excellence quality products in the Italian food and wine sector. TCE allows the application of a rigorous methodology even at a qualitative level. The application of TCE leads to scrutinizing the behavioral assumptions that represent the background of the analyzed transactions and that might generate the transaction costs. The application of TCE drives to qualitatively assess the degree of intensity (high, medium, and low) of the main variables (uncertainty, complexity, and asset specificity) that generate the transaction costs. Such qualitative measurement explains the foundations of production and transaction organizational and governance structure, according to criteria explained by the work of Ronald Coase and Oliver Williamson, both Noble Prize Laureates in Economics.

The application of TCE analysis to five selected high-excellence food and wine products (Parmigiano Reggiano, Amarone della Valpolicella, Prosecco wine, Prosciutto di San Daniele, Mozzarella di Bufala Campana) has shown why and how the organizational structure that governs the production and transaction processes is a common structure, transversal to all products. The optimal governance structure is represented by the Consortium, the "hybrid" institutional form, positioned between neoclassical markets and internal organization and coordinating activities that generate transaction costs of a medium entity. Those TC are generated because the degree of uncertainty, complexity, and asset specificity increases when regulating high-quality/high-excellence products. The input and output quality pursuit, the regulation of identity and product characteristics, the need for careful certification, the implementation of traditional processes and the preservation of traditional knowledge, and the constant monitoring of national and international markets are just a few examples of activities that increase the degree, intensity, and amount of transaction costs.

The Consortia usually coordinate activities through the definition and application of a set of rules, contained in the "*Disciplinare*" that define high qualitative standards of production and regulate the achievement of those high qualitative standards. In this perspective, the sustainability matrix as based on the three (economic, environmental, and social) pillars in the UN definition is not only a driver to achieve high-excellence but is per se achieved by the implementation and by the pursuit of high excellency agri-food production. Sustainability is both a goal and an instrument in the case of the production of Italian high excellence food and wine products. The uncertainty, complexity, and asset specificity of the transactions are impacted by the requirement to implement sustainability. At the same time, millenary production practices, traditional knowledge, and innovative methods turn out to be sustainable, as embodied in the quality features that characterize the high excellency products. In addition, the Consortia are able to incorporate and efficiently minimize the sustainability-driven TC within the hybrid structure organization.

Sustainability is expressed in different ways in the five case studies considered. Sustainability rests mainly on the environmental pillar in the cases of Amarone della Valpolicella and Parmigiano Reggiano. It is based on the social pillar, with a strong ethical connotation, in the cases of Mozzarella di Bufala Campana and Prosecco and has implications of economic sustainability in the case of Prosciutto of San Daniele. More precisely, for each analyzed case study, the pursuit and achievement of sustainability requirements are based on interactions among the three pillars, as clearly represented in Figure 8.1.

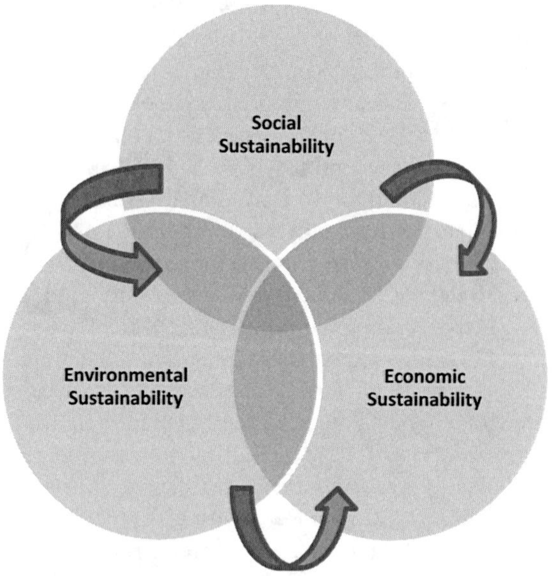

Figure 8.1 Sustainability Pillars

Source: Adapted from Redalpi Group Report[1]

A. Social–Environmental: Environmental Justice, Natural Resources Stewardship Globally and Locally
B. Social-Economic: Social Corporate Responsibility, Business Ethics, Fair Trade, Workers' Rights Protection
C. Economic-Environmental: Energy Efficiency, Efficient Exploitation of Natural Capital and Ecosystem Services

3. Hints for further research

The work has used the economic theory as an interpretative key of the interrelation between excellence and sustainability in the production of selected Italian agri-food products. The goal aimed at providing the reader with a qualitative analysis toolkit that is easily assimilable at a conceptual and intuitive level, but rigorous in its approach, given the scientific nature of the economic theory. Further research could adopt the same methodological framework and apply it for the analysis of important high-excellence Italian food and wine products that were not included in the selection presented in the present work.[2]

Besides, the analyzed phenomena can be interpreted from other perspectives and can be read in keys other than economic science, although they can provide interesting insights for further economic analysis. In this perspective, an important empirical regularity or, in terms of economics, a key variable to add to the further analysis, together with excellence and sustainability, is the historical dimension of the products analyzed. In what follows some historical and literary evidence is reported.

Varro in "*De Rustica*" (first century BC), for instance, describes the Gauls as the greatest experts in the processing and preservation of pork meat and reports that hams from Po Valley Gaul were imported to Rome. The current territory of the Po Valley was inhabited before the Roman colonization by Gauls-Celtic populations. This corresponds to the area where Parma ham is still produced.

Cato the "Censor" in the "*Liber de agri cultura*", dated around the 160 BC, writes about a delicious method of preservation of pork legs and describes a production technique that is remarkably similar to the procedural production steps used nowadays. History tells us that even earlier, as early as the fifth century BC, in the Etruscan Padana the pork legs preserved by salting were traded with the rest of Italy and Greece. Also, the area of San Daniele del Friuli was inhabited by Celtic populations before Roman conquer, and the archaeological investigations of the Church of San Daniele in Castello indicate that the use of pigs for food dates back as the protohistoric period between 1100 and 800 BC. Pig farming and slaughtering developed during the Middle Ages, when the village of San Daniele was ruled by a feudal patriarch for over seven centuries, which contributed to much of its success and prosperity since the patriarch granted San Daniele the privilege of holding a market, with the earliest evidence of a free trade zone dating back to 1063 BC. This privilege was later confirmed by Frederick II is 1232 after Christ (AC) Virgil is 70/19 BC).[3]

The Poet Virgil (70–19 BC) passing through the Conegliano Valdobbiadene area had witnessed that (more than 2000 years ago) vines were grown on the hills of Conegliano Valdobbiadene. He wrote "*Adspice, ut, autrum silvestris raris sparsit lambrusca recemis*" (look at how the wild vine, the Lambrusca, has covered the cave here and there with its clusters). A few years later the poet writes: "*Lentae textunt umbracula vites*" (the flexible vines weave light shadows). This testifies, if not the existence of Prosecco wine, at least a millenary, long-lasting tradition of vine cultivation (Von Peschke and Feldman, 2001)

In Italian "Amarone" is a superlative adjective and means "very bitter". The mention to a "bitter wine" is contained in the work of the Latin poet Catullus in the Carme n. 27 (written around 49 BC). The poet claims "*calices amariores*" (more bitter glasses). Moreover, in the work "The Lives of the Twelve Caesars" (first century AD), Suetonius writes about the emperor Augustus that "*Et maxime delectatus est Raetico, neque temere interdiu bibit*". The emperor particularly liked drinking Rhaetian wine (i.e., the wine produced in the area of the Adige valleys where Amarone, among other wines, is produced nowadays, among other wines) but rarely drank it during the day. The transformation of milk into Parmigiano-Reggiano is still based on artisanal technology, linked to the empirical experience of cheesemakers and the observance of centuries-old customs and traditions. From numerous historiographical sources, it is noted that the most significant contribution to the origin of the product is ascribable to the Benedictine abbeys, which in medieval times contributed to the reclamation of the area concerned and spread technical knowledge of milk processing handed down over the centuries.

For the Mozzarella di Bufala Campana, the first historical documents mentioning the existence of the cheese, appear in the twelfth century. The documents report that the monks of the monastery of San Lorenzo in Capua had the habit to offer a cheese called either "mound" or provatura (when smoked), accompanied by a piece of bread, to the pilgrims who went every year in procession to the church of the Convent[4] (Alicandri, 1915).

Those "random" examples of traces of high-excellency Italian agri-food dating back to the remote past tell us about foods and wines that have conquered and fascinated emperors and kings, pilgrims and writers and contributed to the prosperity of populations then as they are doing now. But it also tells us a story about ancient agri-food traditions and values that have been handed down to the present day (see Kahnemann and Tversky, 2000). The historical component emphasizes the importance of understanding production and consumption habits. On the one hand, production has evolved and innovated technologically, maintaining and researching the roots of sustainability that give excellence to the product itself. On the demand side, preferences for the product and the habit of consuming it seem unchanged for millennia. This applies not only to consumers, who have formed a (probably exogenous, see Becker and Stiegler, 1977) preference for consumption through social, family, and traditional habit and education, but also to consumers alien to such anthropo-historical roots (such as consumers in foreign markets), who have developed a strong (probably exogenous) preference and taste for the consumption of excellent agri-food products. Amarone wine pleases the American tycoon today as it pleased Emperor Augustus 2000 years ago; Prosciutto di San Daniele del Friuli is appreciated by the Japanese consumer today as it was appreciated by Emperor Frederick II, Stupor mundi in Middle Ages. By considering the "*Made in Italy*" effect exogenous, an attempt at explanation could be traced back to the essence of the concept of sustainability. The term sustainability, in the literal sense, carries with it the idea of durability. Today, the meaning of the term, interpreted by the UN, lies on economic, social, and environmental bases, inextricably linked for present adequate use and future transmission of resources. Even in the times of the ancient Romans, of Catullus, as of Varro, of Frederick II as of the Saracens who brought the buffaloes to Italy in the early Middle Ages, agri-food production was a source of income; of social cohesion, through work in abbeys and villages; and a source of conservative use of biodiverse and environmental factors of production. Sustainable production is a historical key that has made it possible to consume and produce output of excellence, which today, as then, seeks the sustainable matrix, declined and implemented in a modern key, for the transmission of wealth, knowledge, culture, and excellence to future generations.

Obviously, much work has to be produced along those lines.

Notes

1 Available at www.redalpi.com/web/sustainability/.

2 The number and variety of Italian high excellency food and wine products are very large. Among the best-known products at the national level, we can mention the Parma raw ham, obtained through a precise methodology respecting the tradition. The Parma ham must successfully passes nine stages of processing which end with a further careful examination and with the "coronation" by the fire with the well-known brand. The typical production area includes the territory of the province of Parma, south of the Via Emilia, at a distance of no less than 5 kilometers from it, up to an altitude of no more than 900 meters above sea level and bordered to the east by the course of the river Enza and to the west by the course of the river Stirone. An essential condition for obtaining Parma ham is that processing takes place in factories located in the typical production area due to the climatic-environmental conditions that play an important role in achieving the final organoleptic characteristics, together with the traditional processing system. The pig destined to become 'Prosciutto di Parma' must have precise characteristics concerning the area of origin (11 regions of northern and central Italy) and the breed; only in the presence of these requirements, certified by the documentation, and tattoo affixed by the breeder can it be sent for slaughter, provided it is over 9 months of age and weighs at least 145 kg. This short summary wants to highlight procedural similarities and governance (through the Prosciutto di Parma Consortium) with the selected case studies. The lists of high excellence products is very long and includes Aceto Balsamico di Modena, Aceto Balsamico di Reggio Emilia, Mortadella di Bologna IGP, Bresaola della Valtellina IGP, Speck dell' Alto Adige IGP, Zampone di Modena IGP, Pecorino Romano, Grana Padano DOP, Gorgonzola DOP, Olio Toscano Igp, Olio della Riviera Ligure DOP, Robiola di Roccaverano, Taleggio DOP, Toma Piemontese, Pecorino Sardo DOP, Pecorino Siciliano DOP, Pecorino Toscano DOP, Salsiccia e Soppressata di Calabria, Prosciutto di Norcia, Prosciutto di Carpegna, and Pancetta Piacentina, just to mention a very few. They are all PDO-certified products. The products list also includes high excellence wines like Chianti, Soave, Brunello di Montalcino, Cannonau di

Sardegna, Barolo, Nero d'Avola, Negramaro, Montepulciano d'Abruzzo, Aglianico Beneventano, and Franciacorta as selected examples, not to mention the plethora of liquors including several kinds of Grappa.

3 https://prosciuttosandaniele.it/la-nostra-storia/.

4 The origins of mozzarella are directly linked to the introduction of buffaloes in Italy. One of the most accredited hypotheses claims that the diffusion in southern Italy took place in the Norman period, starting from Sicily where the buffaloes had been brought towards the end of the tenth century, following the invasions of the Saracens and the Moors.

References

Alicandri, M. (1915). Il Mazzone Il Mazzone nell'antichità e nei tempi presenti.

Becker, G.S. and G.J. Stigler (1977). De Gustibus Non Est Disputandum. *American Economic Review*, 67(2), 76–90.

Kahneman, D. and A. Tversky (2000). *Choices, Values and Frames*. Princeton, NJ: Princeton University Press.

Von Peschke, H.P. and W. Feldmann (2001). *La cucina dell'antica Roma*. Milano: Tommasi.

Index

Note: Page numbers in *italics* indicate a figure and page numbers in **bold** indicate a table on the corresponding page. Page numbers followed by "n" indicate a note.